The 98-Day Takeover

B.O.S.S.

Becoming Our Superior Self

Published by Grin and Barrett Publishing

ISBN: 979-8-9954584-1-8

Cover design by JP Armstrong

Printed in the United States of America

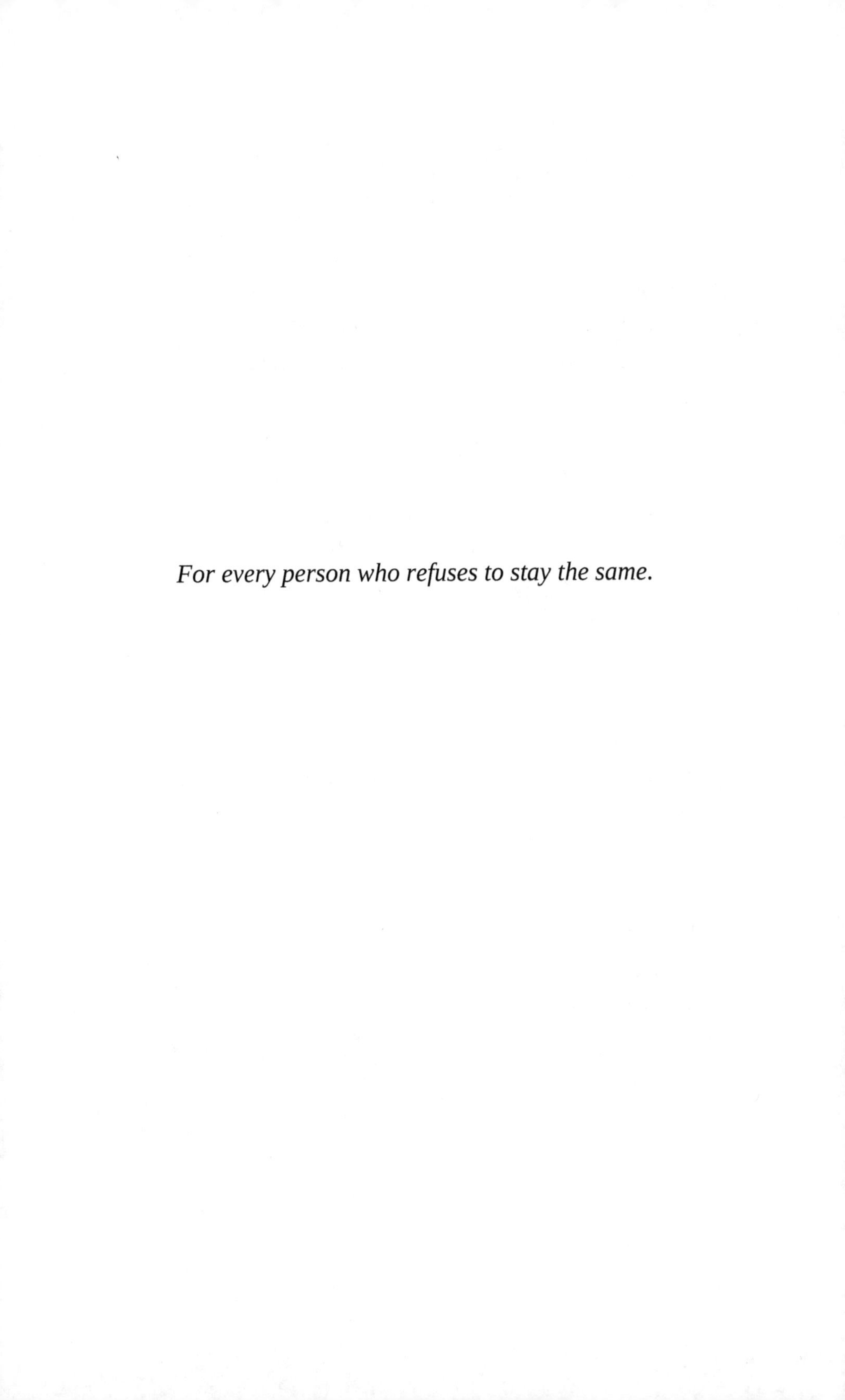

For every person who refuses to stay the same.

CONTENTS

Introduction

    Phase 1: Foundations of the Superior Self

    Phase 2: Developing Real-Time Self-Awareness

    Phase 3: The Identity Mirror

    Phase 4: Unlock the Secrets to Understanding

    Phase 5: Core Values and Decision Making

    Phase 6: Discovering and Fueling Your True Passion

    Phase 7: Security in the Sense of Self

    Phase 8: Stepping Into Authentic Leadership

    Phase 9: Mastering Habits for Success

    Phase 10: The Power of Mindset

    Phase 11: Building Resilience and Grit

    Phase 12: Purpose, Passion, and Calling

    Phase 13: Empowering Relationships and Communication

    Phase 14: Legacy and Lifelong Growth

    Phase 15: The 98-Day Integration

Conclusion

Acknowledgments

About the Author

Also by the Author

Notes

Introduction

You picked up this book for a reason. Something inside you knows that where you are right now isn't where you're supposed to stay. Maybe you've felt it for a while, that quiet pull toward something bigger, something more aligned with who you actually are. That feeling isn't random. It's a signal worth listening to.

Becoming Our Superior Self, what we call B.O.S.S., starts with one conscious decision: to grow. Not to be perfect. Not to have everything figured out. Just to grow. And the fact that you're here, holding these pages, means you've already made that decision. That matters more than you think.

This is the 98-Day Superior Self Takeover. It's a structured, 14-week system built specifically for working professionals, entrepreneurs, and young adults who are tired of reading self-help books that sound great but don't actually change anything. You've probably been there before. You finish a book feeling fired up, you highlight a few lines, maybe you even tell a friend about it, and then two weeks later, nothing has changed. Life goes back to the same patterns. The same habits. The same version of you.

That's not what this is.

This takeover was designed to move you past inspiration and into actual transformation. Every single week has a clear focus. Every single day has a specific action. You won't be left wondering what to do next, because the system tells you exactly where to put your energy. The structure is the point. Without it, change stays theoretical. With it, change becomes real.

Think about a hypothetical person, say a 34-year-old marketing manager named Darius. He's good at his job, respected by his team, and by most outside measures, doing well. But every Sunday night, he feels a low-level dread he can't quite name. He's been meaning to work on himself for years. He's bought the books, listened to the podcasts, even started a journal once or twice. But nothing stuck. The problem wasn't Darius's desire to change. The problem was that he never had a system that held him accountable day by day. He needed a roadmap, not just a destination. That's exactly what this takeover gives you.

The 98 days are broken into two major phases. The first seven weeks focus on self-discovery, covering things like self-awareness, identity, understanding how you see the world, your core values, your passions, your sense of security, and what drives you at the deepest level. The second seven weeks, what we call B.O.S.S. 2.0, shift into high-performance territory: leadership, habits, mindset, resilience, purpose, relationships, and legacy. Each phase builds on the one before it. You can't lead others well if you don't know yourself. You can't build strong habits if you haven't examined the automatic ones already running your life.

Two tools will guide you through this entire process. The first is the Visual Progress Map, a week-by-week tracker that lets you see exactly where you are and how far you've come. There's something powerful about checking off a box and seeing your progress laid out in front of you. It turns an abstract idea like "personal growth" into something you can actually see and measure. The second tool is the Centering Breath Takeover. Before you start each day's work, you'll use a simple breathing practice to clear your head and bring your focus into the present. Sit comfortably, close your eyes, and take five slow, deep breaths. With each inhale, draw in clarity. With each exhale, let go of whatever's pulling your attention away. It takes less than two minutes, and it changes the quality of everything that follows.

These aren't gimmicks. They're anchors.

Each week also ends with a recap and a short checkpoint quiz, so you can measure what you've actually absorbed before moving forward. Growth without reflection is just motion. The checkpoints turn motion into progress.

Most people don't fail to change because they lack the desire. They fail because they don't have a clear path. They wake up wanting to be better, but by 9 a.m., the emails are piling up, the meetings are starting, and the version of themselves they wanted to become gets pushed to tomorrow. Again.

This takeover fixes that by replacing vague intentions with specific daily micro-actions. A micro-action is a small, precise step you can take in a few minutes that moves you forward in a meaningful way. Small doesn't mean insignificant. Small, done consistently over 98 days, becomes something completely different. It becomes a new identity.

The roadmap works like this. Each week has a theme. Each day within that week has a focused lesson, a reflection prompt, a challenge, and a micro-action. You read the lesson. You sit with the reflection. You take the challenge. You do the micro-action. That's it. You don't need to spend hours on this. You need to show up consistently, day after day, and do the small thing in front of you.

Week one, for example, centers on the idea of becoming your superior self. Day one is about setting your intention for the entire takeover. Your challenge that day is simple: write one sentence that captures what you're committing to during these 98 days. Something like, "During B.O.S.S., I am committed to being honest with myself." Then your micro-action is to say that sentence out loud, or share it with someone you trust. That's it. One sentence. Said out loud. But that one act shifts something. It moves your commitment from a private thought to a real declaration. It makes it harder to ignore.

Day two focuses on the power of choice. Your challenge is to list three habits you want to keep and three you want to change. Your micro-action is to pick one habit from the "change" list and plan one small step you'll take tomorrow. Not a complete overhaul. One step. Day three asks you to track a recurring pattern in your behavior for the next three days, writing down when it shows up and how you respond. By the time you reach day seven, the weekly recap, you've already started to see yourself more clearly than you did when you started.

This is how the system works. It doesn't ask you to transform overnight. It asks you to show up today and do the next thing. Then tomorrow, do the next thing after that. The roadmap removes the paralysis of not knowing where to start, because you always know exactly where to start: right here, right now, with today's action.

Self-discovery starts with an honest inventory of where you are. Your habits, your routines, the beliefs you carry around without questioning them. Most people skip this step because it's uncomfortable. Looking at yourself clearly, without making excuses or assigning blame, takes real courage. But you can't change what you won't face. And the good news is that awareness itself is already a form of change. The moment you clearly see a pattern, it starts to lose its grip on you.

Week two of the takeover goes deeper into self-awareness, specifically the kind that happens in real time. On day eight, you'll set a timer three times throughout the day. Each time it goes off, you pause and check in: what am I thinking right now? How am I feeling? What am I doing? That's it. No judgment. No fixing. Just noticing. The practice sounds almost too simple, but most people go entire days, sometimes entire years, on autopilot. They react instead of respond. They run old programs without realizing it. Three check-ins a day starts to break that pattern.

Day nine introduces emotional triggers. Everyone has them. The things that make you snap, shut down, or spiral. The takeover doesn't ask you to eliminate your triggers. It asks you to get curious about them. When you feel triggered, pause and take three deep breaths before you react. Then later, write down what happened and what might be underneath it. Often, what looks like anger is actually fear. What looks like laziness is actually anxiety. Naming the real thing gives you power over it.

By day eleven, you're working on automatic habits, those behaviors you do without thinking. Your challenge that day is to replace one automatic habit with one intentional action. Maybe you reach for your phone the moment you wake up. What if, just for today, you replaced that with two minutes of stillness or a few lines in a journal? After you make the change, notice how you feel. That noticing is data. It tells you what the old habit was actually doing for you, and whether the new one serves you better.

Day twelve covers boundaries. Protecting your time and energy isn't selfish. It's necessary. Your challenge is to say no to one thing that drains you. Just one. And then notice how it feels to honor your own needs. For a lot of people, especially high-achieving professionals, this is harder than it sounds. They've built entire identities around being available, being helpful, being the person who never says no. But a person who can't protect their energy can't sustain their performance. Boundaries aren't walls. They're the structure that makes everything else possible.

The Core Lesson: Progress Over Perfection

There's one idea that runs through every single day of this takeover, and it's worth naming clearly right here at the start: progress matters more than perfection.

Perfection is a trap. It convinces you to wait until you're ready, until you have more time, until things calm down, until you feel more confident. But that moment never comes. The people who actually transform their lives aren't the ones who waited until conditions were perfect. They're the ones who started anyway, showed up imperfectly, and kept going.

This takeover is built around that truth. You're going to have days where you skip the micro-action. Days where you feel like nothing is changing. Days where the old version of you shows up louder than ever. That's normal. It's part of the process. The takeover doesn't ask you to be perfect. It asks you to keep showing up.

Week three of the takeover is where identity work begins. On day fifteen, your challenge is to write ten words that describe your true self, not your job title, not your role as a parent or a partner, but your actual qualities and values. Words like "curious," "resilient," "honest," "creative." Then share that list with someone you trust. This exercise seems simple, but for many people it's surprisingly hard. They've spent so long defining themselves by what they do that they've lost touch with who they are.

Consider a hypothetical scenario: imagine someone like Andre, a 41-year-old who spent fifteen years building his career in finance. His identity was his title. When a restructuring eliminated his position, he didn't just lose a job. He felt like he lost himself. Through the kind of identity work this takeover walks you through, he started to see that his real strengths, his ability to stay calm under pressure, his love of problem-solving, his loyalty to the people around him, had nothing to do with a company name on his business card. His identity was bigger than any title. That realization didn't happen overnight. It happened through daily reflection, one small step at a time.

Day sixteen asks you to look at the layers of your identity: the family you grew up in, the culture you came from, the beliefs you absorbed before you were old enough to question them. Your challenge is to have a real conversation with a family member or close friend about how your upbringing shaped you. This isn't about blame. It's about clarity. Understanding where your patterns came from is how you decide which ones to keep and which ones to leave behind.

Day seventeen focuses on your circle of influence. The people around you shape you more than most people realize. Their habits, their attitudes, their expectations all seep into how you see yourself and what you think is possible. Your challenge that day is to reach out to someone who inspires you and thank them for their influence. And your micro-action is to pay attention to how your energy changes around different people. Some people lift you. Some people drain you. Knowing the difference is important information.

Day nineteen gets to one of the most powerful practices in the entire takeover: rewriting the stories you tell about yourself. Most people carry old narratives that stopped being true a long time ago. "I'm bad with money." "I'm not a leader." "I'm not disciplined enough." These stories feel like facts, but they're not. They're interpretations. And interpretations can be changed. Your challenge is to take one limiting story and rewrite it as a new affirmation. Then say it out loud. Notice how you feel when you do. That feeling of awkwardness or disbelief is normal. It means the new story is bumping up against the old one. Keep saying it anyway.

The main lesson of this entire book is that small, consistent actions compounded over 98 days create a momentum that's hard to stop. One micro-action seems insignificant. Ninety-eight of them, stacked one on top of the other, become a completely different life. That's not a motivational slogan. It's how change actually works. The brain builds new neural pathways through repetition. Habits form through consistent behavior, not through grand gestures. Identity shifts through accumulated evidence, not through single moments of inspiration.

By the time you reach day 98, you won't just think differently about yourself. You'll have 98 days of proof that you can do hard things. You'll have a track record of showing up, even when it was inconvenient. You'll have replaced automatic behaviors with intentional ones. You'll have examined your identity, questioned your assumptions, set boundaries, sought feedback, and built new habits from the ground up. You won't just be reading about a better version of yourself. You'll be living as that person.

This takeover covers everything from self-awareness and identity to leadership, resilience, purpose, and legacy. It's comprehensive because real transformation is comprehensive. You can't fix your career while ignoring your relationships. You can't build confidence while running on broken habits. Everything is connected, and this system treats it that way.

Before you move into week one, take five minutes right now to do the Intention Setting exercise. Get a pen and a piece of paper. Write down what you hope to gain from these 98 days. Be specific. Don't write "I want to be better." Write what better actually looks like for you. More confidence in meetings? Clearer boundaries with your time? A sense of purpose that doesn't depend on your job title? Write it down. Then write your "why." Why does this matter to you now? What changes if you do this? What stays the same if you don't?

Then write your one-sentence commitment. Say it out loud. That's your starting line.

The 98-Day Superior Self Takeover begins right now, with exactly who you are today. That's enough to start.

Phase 1: Foundations of the Superior Self

The Power of Choice and Vision

Every single day, you make hundreds of choices. Most of them happen so fast you barely notice. What to check first when you wake up. Whether to speak up in a meeting or stay quiet. Whether to push through discomfort or retreat to what's comfortable. These moments feel small. They're not. Each one is a vote for the person you're becoming, or the person you're staying as.

That's the core idea behind everything in Phase 1. You are not a passenger watching your life happen to you. You are the driver. And the wheel is always in your hands, even when it doesn't feel that way.

Most people don't think of their daily decisions as building something. They think of choices as isolated moments, each one unconnected to the next. But that's not how it works. Every time you choose to stay consistent with a value, you strengthen it. Every time you choose the easier path over the right one, you reinforce that too. Over weeks and months, these choices stack up into something very real: your character, your habits, and ultimately, your life.

This isn't about pressure. It's about power. Once you understand that your choices are shaping you constantly, you stop feeling like life is something that happens to you and start seeing it as something you're actively building.

The first thing Phase 1 asks you to do is get clear on your vision. Not a vague hope. Not a wish. A specific, written picture of who you want to be when these 98 days are done. This matters more than most people realize. Research on goal-setting consistently shows that people who write down specific goals are far more likely to follow through than those who keep their goals in their head. Writing it down makes it real. It moves the vision from abstract to concrete.

Think about someone like Priya, a 29-year-old project manager who started this takeover with a vague sense that she wanted to "be more confident." That's a fine starting point, but it's too blurry to act on. Through the Intention Setting process, she got specific. Her written vision became: "By the end of 98 days, I speak up in every team meeting with at least one clear contribution, and I stop apologizing for taking up space." That's something she could actually measure. That's something she could wake up and work toward. The specificity changed everything about how she approached each day.

Your vision doesn't have to be dramatic. It doesn't have to involve a career change or a complete lifestyle overhaul. It just has to be honest and specific. What does your superior self actually look like? How does that person carry themselves? What do they say yes to? What do they say no to? What habits do they have that you don't have yet?

Once you have your vision, you anchor it with the Intention Setting Ritual. This is a short, written process you do right now, before you go any further. Here's exactly how to do it.

Grab a pen and a blank piece of paper or open a fresh note on your phone. At the top, write the date. Then answer these three questions in writing, not in your head. First: what do I want to gain from these 98 days? Be specific. Name the actual change you want to see. Second: why does this matter to me right now? Not why it should matter in theory, but why it matters to you personally, at this specific point in your life. Third: who do I need to become to make this happen? Write one sentence that captures the version of yourself you're working toward.

That third answer becomes your intention statement. It's the sentence that anchors your entire 98-day takeover. Keep it somewhere you'll see it every day. Put it on a sticky note on your mirror. Set it as your phone wallpaper. Write it at the top of every journal entry. The repetition isn't cheesy. It's strategic. You're training your brain to orient toward this version of yourself instead of defaulting to the old one.

Choice and vision work together in a specific way. The vision gives you direction. The choices give you the daily practice of moving toward it. Without a vision, your choices are random. Without consistent choices, your vision stays a fantasy. The two need each other.

One more thing worth saying here: the vision you write today doesn't have to be perfect. You'll learn more about yourself over the coming weeks, and your understanding of what you want may sharpen. That's fine. What matters is that you start with something written and specific. You can refine it as you go. You can't refine something that doesn't exist yet.

Overcoming Limiting Beliefs

You've set your vision. You know what you're working toward. Now comes the part that most people skip, which is exactly why most people don't change.

Between you and that vision is a layer of beliefs about yourself that you've been carrying for years. Some of those beliefs are accurate and useful. Others are outdated stories you picked up somewhere along the way and never stopped to question. These are your limiting beliefs, and they're the single biggest reason that smart, capable, motivated people stay stuck.

A limiting belief isn't always dramatic. It doesn't always sound like "I'm worthless" or "I'll never succeed." More often, it sounds like something quieter and more reasonable. "I'm just not a morning person." "I've never been good at sticking to things." "People like me don't usually get those kinds of opportunities." These thoughts feel like facts because you've thought them so many times. They're not facts. They're habits of thinking. And like any habit, they can be changed.

The first step is awareness. You can't change a belief you haven't noticed. Most people's limiting beliefs run in the background like software they didn't install on purpose. The beliefs just run, shaping what they try, what they avoid, and what they tell themselves is possible. Bringing those beliefs into conscious awareness is how you start to interrupt the pattern.

Start by paying attention to your self-talk throughout the day. Not in a clinical way, just as an observer. When you're about to try something new, what does your inner voice say? When you make a mistake, how do you talk to yourself about it? When an opportunity comes up, what's the first thought that follows? That inner voice is carrying your belief system. Listening to it carefully tells you a lot about what you actually believe, as opposed to what you think you believe.

Consider a hypothetical scenario: imagine someone like Marcus, a 36-year-old sales director who wanted to start his own consulting business but kept finding reasons to delay. He told himself he was being practical. He was waiting for the right time, the right amount of savings, the right level of certainty. But when he started journaling his self-talk during the takeover, he noticed something. Every time he got close to taking a real step, the same thought appeared: "Who am I to think I can do this?" That one sentence, running quietly in the background, had been stopping him for three years. It wasn't practicality. It was fear dressed up as logic. Naming it gave him something to work with. He couldn't fight a ghost. But he could challenge a specific thought.

Once you've identified a limiting belief, the next step is to challenge it directly. This doesn't mean talking yourself into blind optimism. It means asking honest questions. Where did this belief come from? Is there actual evidence that it's true? Is there evidence that contradicts it? What would I believe about this if I were someone I admire? These questions create a crack in the wall. They let in new possibilities.

The replacement step comes after the challenge. You take the limiting belief and you rewrite it. Not as a fantasy, but as a more accurate and useful statement. "I've never been good at sticking to things" becomes "I haven't built the right system yet, and I'm building one now." "People like me don't usually get those opportunities" becomes "I'm creating the conditions to be ready when opportunities come." The new statement has to feel at least partially believable, or your brain will reject it immediately. Start with something you can genuinely consider possible, even if you don't fully believe it yet.

Self-sabotage is the behavioral side of limiting beliefs. It's what happens when your unconscious belief system starts working against your conscious goals. You set a goal to wake up earlier, and three days in you're hitting snooze again. You commit to a new habit, and then you find yourself doing the old one without even deciding to. You make progress, and then you somehow manage to undo it. This isn't weakness. It's your nervous system protecting what's familiar. Change feels threatening to the part of your brain that equates familiarity with safety. Understanding that doesn't make it okay to stay stuck, but it does make the pattern less mysterious and less personal.

The way to work with self-sabotage is to get specific about how it shows up for you. Everybody's version looks a little different. Some people self-sabotage through procrastination. Others through perfectionism, waiting until something is perfect before they share it or act on it, which means it never goes anywhere. Others do it through busyness, staying so occupied with low-priority tasks that they never get to the things that actually matter. Identify your specific pattern. Write it down. Then design a small, concrete response for the next time it shows up.

For example, if your pattern is procrastination, your response might be: the moment I notice I'm delaying an important task, I'll set a timer for ten minutes and work on it for exactly that long. Ten minutes. No commitment to finish, just to start. That's it. The starting is almost always the hardest part. Once you're in motion, momentum takes over.

There's also the matter of emotional triggers. These are the situations, words, or dynamics that set off a strong emotional reaction in you. When you're triggered, your ability to think clearly drops. You react instead of respond. You say things you regret, make decisions you wouldn't otherwise make, or shut down completely. Triggers aren't character flaws. They're signals pointing toward something unresolved. Getting curious about your triggers, instead of ashamed of them, is one of the most useful things you can do in Phase 1.

When you notice you've been triggered, pause. Take three slow breaths before you say or do anything. Then, later, when you're calm, write down what happened. What was the situation? What did you feel in your body? What thought followed the feeling? What does this remind you of? That last question is often the most revealing. Triggers usually have roots. The coworker who dismisses your ideas might be triggering something that started long before that meeting room. Understanding the root doesn't excuse the reaction, but it does give you something to work with.

Your inner narrative is the story you tell about yourself and your life. It's built from years of experiences, feedback you received, comparisons you made, and conclusions you drew. Some of that narrative is accurate and worth keeping. Some of it is a distortion that's been running unchallenged for too long. The work of Phase 1 is to look at that narrative clearly and decide, consciously, which parts you want to carry forward and which parts you're ready to leave behind.

You're not your inner critic. The voice that tells you you're not ready, not smart enough, not disciplined enough, that voice is not the truth about you. It's a pattern. And patterns can be interrupted, redirected, and replaced with something more accurate and more useful.

Growth requires honesty. Not harshness, just honesty. You have to be willing to look at where you are right now, without softening it too much and without catastrophizing it either. The goal isn't to feel bad about where you've been. The goal is to see clearly so you can move forward with your eyes open.

One last thing about limiting beliefs: they don't disappear after you challenge them once. They tend to come back, especially when you're under pressure or trying something new. That's normal. The goal isn't to eliminate the thought forever. The goal is to get faster at recognizing it, quicker at challenging it, and more practiced at choosing a different response. Over time, with repetition, the new response becomes the default. That's how beliefs actually change: through consistent, repeated practice, not through a single moment of insight.

Your Starting Point: Actions to Take Right Now

Everything you've read in this chapter only becomes useful when it moves from the page into your actual life. The three actions below are specific, concrete, and designed to take less than twenty minutes total. Do them in order. Don't skip ahead.

The first action is the Centering Breath Exercise. Before you do anything else, sit comfortably in a chair with both feet flat on the floor. Close your eyes. Take five slow, deep breaths. With each inhale, breathe in through your nose for a count of four and imagine drawing in clarity and focus. With each exhale, breathe out through your mouth for a count of six and release whatever tension or distraction you're carrying. Don't rush this. Five breaths, done slowly and deliberately, takes about ninety seconds. This isn't filler. It's a reset. It moves your nervous system out of reactive mode and into a state where you can actually think. Do this exercise every single morning before you start the day's takeover work. It takes less than two minutes and it changes the quality of everything that follows.

The second action is to write your "why." Open a journal, a notebook, or a blank document. At the top, write today's date. Then write your answers to these three questions: What do I want to be different at the end of these 98 days? Why does that change matter to me right now, specifically? What has it cost me to stay the same until now? Don't overthink this. Write whatever comes up honestly. Aim for at least three to five sentences per question. The goal isn't perfect prose. The goal is clarity. When you're done, read what you wrote out loud to yourself. Hearing your own words spoken aloud makes them feel more real and more binding than reading them silently.

The third action is to write your one-sentence intention and share it. Take the most important thing you wrote in step two and compress it into a single clear sentence. Start it with "During these 98 days, I am committed to..." and finish it with something specific and honest. Then share that sentence with one person you trust. Send a text, say it in person, or read it to someone over a call. If there's no one available right now, say it out loud to yourself in front of a mirror. The act of speaking your commitment out loud, and especially of saying it to another person, changes its status. It's no longer just a private thought. It's a declaration. That shift in status makes it significantly harder to quietly abandon later.

These three actions together take about fifteen to twenty minutes. They're the foundation everything else in this takeover builds on. The vision you've set, the beliefs you've started to examine, and the intention you've declared are your starting materials. The next 97 days are about building something real with them.

Phase 2: Developing Real-Time Self-Awareness

Awareness in the Present Moment

Most of your day is already decided before you consciously choose anything. You wake up and reach for your phone. You sit in a meeting and zone out for ten minutes without noticing. You snap at someone and only realize what happened after the fact. You eat lunch at your desk, scroll through something, and barely taste the food. None of this is a character flaw. It's autopilot, and almost every person alive spends a significant portion of their day running on it.

The problem with autopilot isn't that it exists. Your brain uses it to conserve energy, and that's actually useful for routine tasks. The problem is when autopilot starts making your important decisions for you. When it controls how you respond to stress, how you treat the people around you, how you talk to yourself, and whether you move toward your goals or away from them. That's when it stops being efficient and starts being expensive.

Real-time self-awareness is the skill of catching yourself in the act. Not after the fact, not in a therapy session six months later, but in the actual moment something is happening. It's the ability to notice what you're thinking, feeling, and doing as it unfolds, without immediately judging it or trying to fix it. Just noticing. That noticing is where your power lives.

Think about what it actually means to go through a day on autopilot. You don't register the tension building in your shoulders during a stressful call. You don't notice that your mood shifted after checking your email. You don't catch the moment you started catastrophizing about a project deadline. These things happen, they affect your behavior, and you have no idea they're running the show. Awareness changes that. The second you notice something, you have a choice about what to do with it. Before you notice it, you have no choice at all.

Consider someone like Danielle, a hypothetical 31-year-old operations lead at a mid-sized company. She described herself as "reactive" and couldn't figure out why. She'd leave meetings feeling drained and irritable without knowing what triggered it. She'd send emails she later regretted. She'd commit to things she didn't want to do and then resent the people who asked. When she started doing structured awareness check-ins throughout her day, the patterns became visible almost immediately. She realized she felt most reactive when she hadn't eaten and when she'd gone more than two hours without a break. She noticed that a specific coworker's tone made her defensive before the person even finished a sentence. She saw that she said yes to requests within the first three seconds, before her brain had time to weigh in. None of this was a mystery once she started paying attention. The awareness itself didn't fix everything overnight, but it gave her something she didn't have before: information she could actually use.

The Real-Time Awareness Audit is the core practice of this section, and it's built around one simple tool: a timer. Three times today, set an alarm. Space them out across your day, maybe morning, early afternoon, and late afternoon. When the alarm goes off, stop whatever you're doing for sixty seconds and answer three questions honestly. What am I thinking right now? How am I feeling right now? What am I doing right now? Write the answers down if you can, even just a few words. If you can't write, just pause and answer them in your head.

That's it. Three check-ins. Sixty seconds each.

It sounds almost too simple to matter. But here's what actually happens when you do this consistently. You start to see patterns. You notice that your thinking gets scattered around the same time each day. You realize you're carrying a low-level anxiety that you weren't consciously aware of. You catch yourself mentally rehearsing a difficult conversation while you're supposed to be listening to someone else.

These aren't small discoveries. They're the data points that tell you where your attention actually goes, as opposed to where you think it goes.

The non-judgment piece is critical and worth spending a moment on. When you check in and notice that you've been stewing about something for the past hour, the instinct for most people is to criticize themselves for it. "Why am I still thinking about that? I should be over it." That reaction is counterproductive. The moment you judge what you find, you stop being an observer and start being a critic. And a critic's job is to protect, not to learn. Judgment shuts down curiosity. Non-judgment keeps it open.

What you find during your check-ins isn't good or bad. It's just true. And true information, even uncomfortable true information, is always more useful than a comfortable illusion. Awareness is power precisely because it gives you accurate data about what's actually happening inside you. You can't steer with inaccurate information. You can only steer with what's real.

There's also a habit component to this section that's worth addressing directly. A lot of what you do each day isn't chosen, it's automatic. You follow the same morning sequence without deciding to. You check the same apps in the same order. You respond to stress in the same way you always have. These automatic habits aren't inherently bad. Some of them are genuinely helpful. But you can't evaluate a habit you haven't noticed. The awareness audit gives you the chance to see your automatic behaviors clearly, and then decide whether they're actually serving you.

Pick one automatic habit today and bring deliberate attention to it. Don't try to change it yet. Just watch it happen. Notice what triggers it, what it feels like when you do it, and what follows after. That observation alone starts to loosen the habit's grip. You're moving it from unconscious to conscious, and that shift is the first step toward any real change.

Boundaries are another layer of present-moment awareness that most people overlook. You can't set a boundary you haven't noticed you need. When you feel your energy dropping in a conversation, when you feel resentment building around a commitment, when you feel stretched past your actual capacity, those are signals. They're your body and mind telling you something important. The awareness audit trains you to catch those signals earlier, before they build into something harder to manage.

Practice this today: when something drains your energy, notice it in the moment rather than hours later. You don't have to act on it immediately. Just register it. "This is draining me right now." That noticing is the beginning of being able to do something about it.

Identifying Emotional Triggers

Everyone has them. The colleague who interrupts you in meetings. The tone your manager uses when they're disappointed. The feeling of being left out of a conversation. The moment someone questions your competence in front of others. These things hit differently than ordinary discomfort. They don't just bother you, they set something off. Your chest tightens. Your jaw clenches. You feel a flash of heat or a sudden urge to withdraw. That's a trigger.

A trigger is a strong emotional reaction that feels bigger than the situation seems to call for. That disproportionate quality is actually the most useful thing about it. When your reaction is much larger than the event, it's a signal that the event is touching something older and deeper than the present moment. The current situation is the match. The trigger is the fuel that was already there.

Understanding your triggers isn't about becoming emotionally flat or never reacting to anything. It's about knowing what sets you off so you can choose your response instead of just firing one automatically. The difference between someone who reacts and someone who responds isn't that the second person doesn't feel anything. It's that they've built a small but crucial gap between the feeling and the action. That gap is where your best decisions live.

The root of most triggers isn't the present situation. It's a past experience that the present situation is echoing. Someone dismissing your idea in a meeting might be triggering a childhood memory of not being heard. Feeling left out of a decision might be connecting to an old wound around belonging. Being questioned on your competence might be touching a fear of failure that was planted years ago. This doesn't mean you have to spend months in therapy to manage your triggers. But it does mean that getting curious about what's underneath a strong reaction is far more useful than just trying to suppress the reaction itself.

Think about a hypothetical scenario involving someone like Kevin, a 38-year-old team lead who noticed he got unusually tense whenever a project he owned was discussed in group settings without him being consulted first. He'd feel a sharp spike of irritation that he'd try to hide, but it leaked out anyway, through clipped responses and a closed-off posture. When he actually sat with the feeling instead of pushing it away, he traced it back to years of being overlooked in a family where his older siblings got most of the attention and decision-making power. The workplace situation wasn't really about the project. It was about feeling invisible. Once Kevin named that connection, he didn't automatically stop feeling triggered, but he stopped being confused by it. And that clarity gave him the ability to pause before reacting, take a breath, and ask himself whether his response was coming from the present moment or from something much older. That question alone changed how he showed up in those situations.

The physical sensation of a trigger is one of the most reliable ways to catch it early. Emotions don't just live in your head. They show up in your body first. A tight chest, a clenched jaw, a sinking feeling in your stomach, heat rising in your face, a sudden urge to leave the room. These physical signals arrive before you've consciously registered what you're feeling. Learning to read your body's early warning system gives you more time to choose your response before the reaction is already out of your mouth.

Today, pick one trigger you're aware of. It doesn't have to be your biggest or most complicated one. Just one you recognize. Write down the following four things about it. First, describe the situation that typically sets it off in one or two sentences. Second, describe exactly where you feel it in your body and what it feels like physically. Third, write down the thought or story that usually follows the physical sensation. Fourth, ask yourself what this situation might remind you of from earlier in your life. You don't need a definitive answer to that last question. Just sit with it and write whatever comes up honestly.

When you actually feel triggered today, use this sequence before you respond. The moment you notice the physical signal, stop. Take three slow breaths, inhaling for four counts and exhaling for six. Don't say anything yet. Don't send the message yet. Don't make the decision yet. Just breathe. Those three breaths create the gap between feeling and action. They give your thinking brain time to come back online after the emotional reaction has fired. After the three breaths, ask yourself one question: "Is my response right now coming from this situation, or from something older?" You don't have to answer perfectly. Just asking the question shifts your state.

Triggers aren't character flaws. They're not proof that you're too sensitive or too emotional or not professional enough. They're information about where you've been hurt, where you have unmet needs, and where growth is available to you. The people who manage their emotional reactions best aren't the ones who feel less. They're the ones who know themselves well enough to work with what they feel rather than against it.

One more thing worth saying: you're not trying to eliminate your triggers. That's not a realistic or even desirable goal. The aim is to shrink the gap between being triggered and choosing your response. Over time, with consistent practice, that gap gets wider. You get faster at noticing. You get better at pausing. You get more skilled at choosing. That's the actual work, and it's available to you starting with the very next trigger you encounter.

The Self-Talk Audit

There's a voice in your head that's been talking to you your entire life. It comments on everything you do. It narrates your failures, second-guesses your decisions, compares you to other people, and has an opinion about nearly every situation you walk into. Most people are so used to this voice that they've stopped noticing it. They've started treating it like the truth.

It's not the truth. It's a habit.

Your self-talk is the internal commentary running in the background of your mind throughout the day. Some of it is neutral and practical. "I need to send that email before noon." "I should eat something." But a significant portion of most people's self-talk is negative, critical, and often wildly inaccurate. "I'm going to mess this up." "They probably think I'm incompetent." "I should be further along by now." "Why can't I just get it together?" These thoughts feel like assessments. They feel like honest evaluations of reality. But they're not. They're patterns, built up over years of repetition, and like all patterns, they can be changed.

The reason self-talk matters so much is that your brain takes it seriously. When you tell yourself you're going to mess something up, your brain starts looking for evidence that you're right. When you tell yourself you're not disciplined enough, your brain interprets every small slip as confirmation. This is called confirmation bias, and your inner critic is extremely good at exploiting it. The stories you tell about yourself don't just reflect your reality. Over time, they shape it.

Think about a hypothetical scenario: imagine someone like Simone, a 33-year-old graphic designer who wanted to pitch her own freelance clients but kept holding back. She told herself she wasn't ready, that other designers were more talented, that she'd probably embarrass herself in a sales conversation. When she started writing down her self-talk during the takeover, she was genuinely surprised by how relentless it was. The inner critic wasn't just showing up when things went wrong. It was there every time she opened her laptop, every time she looked at someone else's work, every time she got close to taking a real step forward. She'd been living with this running commentary for so long that she'd stopped hearing it as commentary. She'd started hearing it as reality. Writing it down made it visible. And visible things can be questioned.

The Self-Talk Audit has three steps. The first is to catch the thought. This requires the same kind of present-moment awareness you practiced in the first section of this chapter. Throughout your day, pay attention to what your inner voice is saying, especially in moments of challenge, comparison, or discomfort. When you notice a negative thought, don't argue with it yet. Just write it down exactly as it appeared. "I'm terrible at this." "I always overthink everything." "Nobody takes me seriously." Get it out of your head and onto paper.

The second step is to question the thought. Once it's written down, ask these specific questions about it. Is this thought actually true, or does it just feel true? What evidence would I need to see to prove this thought is accurate? Is there evidence that contradicts it? Would I say this to someone I care about who was in the same situation? That last question is often the most clarifying. Most people are far harsher with themselves than they'd ever be with a friend. Recognizing that double standard starts to loosen the thought's authority.

The third step is to rewrite the thought as a more accurate and useful statement. Not a fake, over-the-top affirmation that your brain will immediately reject. A grounded, honest reframe that you can actually believe, even partially. "I'm terrible at this" becomes "I'm still learning this, and I'm getting better with practice." "I always overthink everything" becomes "I think carefully before acting, and I'm learning when to trust my instincts." "Nobody takes me seriously" becomes "I'm building the track record that earns respect, and that takes time." The new statement doesn't have to feel completely true yet. It just has to feel possible. That's enough to start shifting the pattern.

Once you've written your reframed statement, say it out loud. This step matters more than it might seem. Speaking something out loud activates different neural pathways than just reading it silently. It also forces you to hear your own voice deliver the new message, which is different from having the inner critic deliver it. Say it clearly, at a normal volume, as if you're telling it to someone you trust. If it feels awkward, that's fine. Awkward means the new statement is bumping up against the old one. That friction is actually progress.

You are not your inner critic. That voice is a pattern that formed in response to your experiences, your environment, and the feedback you received over years. It served a purpose at some point, usually as a form of self-protection. But it doesn't have to run the show anymore. You can choose a different voice. Not a naive one, not a blindly positive one, but a honest, grounded, supportive one that tells you the truth without tearing you down in the process.

The audit isn't a one-time exercise. It's a daily practice. The more consistently you catch negative self-talk, question it, and replace it, the faster the pattern shifts. You're essentially building a new habit of thought, and like all habits, it strengthens through repetition. Some days the inner critic will be louder than others. That's expected. The goal isn't silence. The goal is to stop taking every word it says at face value.

Your self-talk and your identity are deeply connected. The stories you tell about yourself become the lens through which you see every situation. Change the story, and you change what you're able to see. Change what you're able to see, and you change what you're able to do. That's not a metaphor. That's the actual mechanism through which self-talk shapes behavior, and it's why the audit is one of the most important practices in this entire takeover.

Your Next Move

This chapter covered a lot of ground. You've looked at how autopilot runs your day without your permission. You've examined the roots of your emotional triggers and learned a concrete way to pause before reacting. You've started to see your self-talk for what it actually is: a habit, not a verdict. These three skills, present-moment awareness, trigger recognition, and self-talk reframing, don't operate in isolation. They build on each other. The more you notice your thoughts in real time, the faster you catch a trigger forming. The faster you catch a trigger, the more space you have to choose your words, including the ones you say to yourself.

Real-time self-awareness isn't something you achieve once and keep forever. It's something you practice, and the practice gets sharper the more consistently you show up for it. The 98-Day Superior Self Takeover is built on exactly this kind of compounding. Small actions, done consistently, become skills. Skills, practiced over time, become identity. The person you're becoming through this process isn't someone who never gets triggered or never has a negative thought. It's someone who notices faster, pauses more reliably, and chooses more deliberately. That's a real and meaningful shift.

Take these three specific actions before you move forward.

First, set your three awareness alarms right now. Open your phone, set three timers spaced across today's remaining hours, and label each one "Check In." When each alarm goes off, stop for sixty seconds and write down your answers to the three questions: what am I thinking, how am I feeling, what am I doing. Don't evaluate the answers. Just record them. Do this for the next seven days in a row and look back at what you wrote at the end of the week. The patterns that show up will tell you more about your current default state than any personality test ever could.

Second, identify one specific trigger you experienced in the last week. Write a short description of the situation, what you felt in your body when it happened, the thought that followed the feeling, and one possible connection to something older. Then write out the three-breath pause sequence as if you're writing instructions for yourself: "The next time I feel this trigger, I will stop, take three breaths counting four in and six out, and ask myself whether my reaction is coming from this moment or from something older." Having that written response ready before the trigger happens means you don't have to figure it out in the heat of the moment.

Third, do a full self-talk audit on one negative thought you've noticed recently. Write the thought down exactly as it sounds in your head. Ask the four questioning prompts from this chapter. Then write a reframed version that's honest, grounded, and at least partially believable to you right now. Say the reframed version out loud three times. Then set a reminder on your phone to say it again tomorrow morning, before you start your day. One thought, reframed and repeated, is more powerful than a dozen affirmations you say once and forget.

These three actions are your entry point into everything that builds from here. The self-awareness you develop in Phase 2 becomes the foundation for the identity work, habit building, and leadership development that comes in the weeks ahead. You can't redesign your life from the outside in. It starts here, with knowing what's actually happening inside you, in real time, one moment at a time.

Phase 3: The Identity Mirror

Strip away your job title for a moment. Take away your role as a manager, a founder, a parent, a partner. Remove every label that describes what you do or what you are to other people. What's left?

For a lot of people, that question creates a kind of quiet panic. Not because they don't have an answer, but because they've never actually looked for one. They've spent so much time becoming good at their roles that they stopped paying attention to who they are underneath them. The role became the identity. And when the role changes, which it always eventually does, the identity feels like it's collapsing right along with it.

That's what Phase 3 is about. Not your job. Not your title. Not the version of yourself you perform for other people. The actual you, the one that exists independent of any external label, any career achievement, or any relationship status. Finding that person, understanding what shaped them, and then deciding who you want to become from the inside out is the most important work in this entire takeover.

The two phases you've already completed weren't just warm-up exercises. The self-awareness you built in Phase 2 and the belief work you started in Phase 1 are exactly what make this phase possible. You can't examine your identity clearly if you're still running on autopilot. You can't rewrite your personal story if you haven't learned to catch the old one playing in your head. Everything you've done so far has been building toward this.

Stripping Away the Labels

Think about the last time someone asked you to introduce yourself. What did you say? Most people go straight to their job. "I'm a project manager." "I run a small business." "I work in finance." It's the default answer because it's the easiest one. Your job tells people something concrete about you, something measurable and socially recognizable. But it doesn't actually tell them who you are.

The problem isn't that you have a job or that your career matters to you. Of course it does. The problem is when the job becomes the whole story. When your sense of worth is tied directly to your title, your company, or your performance metrics, you've handed over the keys to your identity to something that can be taken away at any time. Promotions happen. Layoffs happen. Industries shift. Companies close. If your identity lives entirely inside your professional role, you're one bad quarter away from an identity crisis.

Consider a hypothetical scenario: imagine someone like Renata, a 37-year-old senior account director at a marketing agency. She was excellent at her job and knew it. Her whole social life revolved around colleagues. Her confidence came from being the person people called when a client relationship was falling apart. When her agency was acquired and her position was eliminated in the restructuring, she didn't just lose a job. She lost the entire structure she'd been using to understand herself. She'd been so busy being "the account director" that she hadn't thought about who Renata actually was outside of that building. It took her months to start seeing that her real strengths, her ability to read people, her calm under pressure, her genuine curiosity about others, had nothing to do with a company name. Those qualities were hers. They'd always been hers. The job had just been one place she expressed them.

This is what the Identity Mirror Technique is designed to reveal. It's a structured process that helps you see yourself clearly, not through the lens of what you do, but through the lens of who you actually are.

The first step is what's called the Ten Core Qualities Exercise. This is your starting point, and it's more demanding than it looks. You're going to write a list of ten words that describe your true self. Not your job function. Not your role in a family or team. Not what you're good at professionally. Your actual character qualities and values. Words like "loyal," "creative," "honest," "persistent," "curious," "fair," "brave," "warm," "disciplined," "thoughtful." These are the words that describe who you are when no one's watching, when there's no performance review, when there's nothing to prove.

Here's how to do it properly. Set a timer for fifteen minutes. Open your journal or a blank document. At the top, write: "Who am I when no role is attached to me?" Then start writing words. Don't filter them. Don't second-guess them. Just write. Get to twenty words if you can, then narrow it down to the ten that feel most true and most essential. Not the ten you wish were true. Not the ten that sound impressive. The ten that, if someone who knew you deeply were describing you, they'd say, "Yes, that's exactly right."

Once you have your ten words, ask yourself three questions about the list. First: which of these qualities do I express freely in my daily life, and which ones do I suppress? Second: which of these qualities was I expressing even as a child, before the world started telling me who to be? Third: if I built my career and relationships around these ten qualities instead of around a title, what would change?

The answers to those questions are the beginning of real self-knowledge.

Your social circle is part of this picture too, and it's worth examining honestly. The people you spend the most time with have a quiet but significant influence on how you see yourself. Their habits, their language, their expectations, and their limitations all seep into your self-concept over time. Someone who constantly downplays their own ambitions will, without meaning to, create an environment where ambition feels uncomfortable. Someone who's genuinely curious and growth-focused will make you feel more permission to be those things yourself. This isn't about cutting people off. It's about being honest about who you're spending your energy with and what that's doing to your sense of who you are and what's possible for you.

Pay attention this week to how your energy shifts around different people. Notice who makes you feel more like your ten-word self and who makes you feel like you have to shrink or perform. That information matters. You don't have to act on it immediately. But you do need to see it clearly.

There's also the matter of your automatic habits and how they reflect your current identity. Every habit you have is, in a sense, a vote for a particular version of yourself. The habit of checking your phone first thing in the morning is a vote for distraction over intention. The habit of speaking up in meetings is a vote for confidence and contribution. The habit of staying quiet when something bothers you is a vote for avoidance over honesty. When you look at your daily habits as a collection, they tell you a lot about which identity is actually running your life right now, as opposed to the one you want to be living.

Choose one habit today that doesn't reflect the person your ten words describe. Just one. Don't try to overhaul everything at once. Pick the one that feels most out of alignment with your true character and replace it with one intentional action that does reflect who you actually are. Then notice how that small shift feels. That feeling, even if it's just a flicker of something right, is important data.

The work of stripping away labels isn't about rejecting your career or your roles. Those things are real and they matter. It's about making sure they don't own you. Your title is something you have. It's not something you are. The sooner that distinction becomes real to you, the more stable and grounded your sense of self becomes, regardless of what changes around you. And in a 98-day takeover designed to overhaul your life from the inside out, that kind of stability is the foundation everything else gets built on.

Unpeeling Generational Layers

You didn't arrive at your current identity in a vacuum. Long before you chose a career or formed your own opinions, you were absorbing messages about who you should be, what success looks like, what's acceptable to feel, what kind of person earns love and approval, and what happens when you fall short. Those messages came from your family, your culture, your community, and the experiences that shaped your earliest understanding of the world.

Some of what you absorbed was genuinely useful. Values like hard work, loyalty, and integrity often get passed down through families in ways that serve people well for their entire lives. But some of what got passed down was limiting, anxious, or simply outdated. Beliefs about what you're capable of. Rules about how much space you're allowed to take up. Expectations about what kind of life is realistic for someone like you. These inherited patterns often run so deep that they feel like your own thoughts. They're not always your thoughts. Sometimes they're your parents' fears wearing your voice.

Perfectionism is one of the most common examples. A lot of high-achieving professionals carry a relentless drive to get everything right, and they've always assumed it was just part of their personality. But when they trace it back, they often find a parent who expressed love conditionally, through praise for achievement and disappointment for anything less. Or a household where mistakes were treated as shameful rather than instructive. Or a cultural environment where success was the only acceptable outcome because the family had sacrificed too much for failure to be an option. The perfectionism isn't a personality trait. It's a survival strategy that got locked in early and never got updated.

Consider a hypothetical scenario: imagine someone like Daniel, a 32-year-old software engineer whose parents had immigrated and built their entire lives around the idea that education and professional success would give their children security they never had. Daniel grew up understanding, without anyone saying it directly, that anything less than excellence was a kind of betrayal. He became extremely capable and extremely hard on himself. He'd finish a project and immediately move to the next one without acknowledging what he'd done. He couldn't take a compliment without deflecting it. He couldn't rest without feeling guilty. When he started examining where these patterns came from, he didn't find fault with his parents. He found love, and he found fear. Their fear, passed to him as a set of unspoken rules. Understanding that didn't make the patterns disappear overnight, but it gave him something crucial: the ability to decide for himself which parts of that inheritance he wanted to keep and which ones he was ready to consciously set down.

This is the core work of this section. Not therapy. Not blame. Clarity. You're trying to see which parts of your current identity were chosen and which ones were absorbed without your conscious agreement. Once you can see the difference, you get to decide.

Start with this specific exercise. Take a blank page and draw a vertical line down the middle. On the left side, write "Inherited." On the right side, write "Chosen." In the Inherited column, list the beliefs, rules, and expectations about yourself and the world that you absorbed from your family or cultural background. Things like: "Strong people don't ask for help." "Money is hard to come by." "You have to work twice as hard to be taken seriously." "Emotions are private." "Your worth depends on your productivity." Don't filter for whether they're true or fair. Just write what you actually absorbed.

Then, for each item in the Inherited column, ask one honest question: does this belief still serve the person I'm trying to become? If yes, move it to the Chosen column. If no, or if you're not sure, put a question mark next to it. The question marks are your working list. Those are the beliefs you're going to consciously examine and decide about, rather than carrying by default.

The next step is to have a real conversation. Pick one person who knew you growing up, a parent, a sibling, an older relative, or a close childhood friend. Tell them you're doing some personal reflection work and ask them one direct question: "What do you think shaped how I see myself and what I expect from life?" Then listen without defending. You're not looking for validation or conflict. You're looking for perspective. What they say might surprise you. It might confirm something you already suspected. Either way, it's information you can use.

After that conversation, write down one specific belief you're ready to consciously change. Not because someone told you to, but because you've looked at it honestly and decided it doesn't fit who you actually want to be. Write the old belief in one sentence. Then write the new belief you're choosing to replace it with. The new belief has to be honest and realistic. It can't be the opposite of the old one just for the sake of it.

It has to be something you can genuinely begin to build evidence for through your daily actions.

For example, if the inherited belief is "asking for help means you're weak," the chosen replacement might be "asking for help is how capable people get better faster." That's not a fantasy. It's a reframe grounded in reality, and it's one you can test immediately by actually asking for help with something this week and observing what happens.

Your past is not your prison. It's your starting point. Understanding what shaped you doesn't lock you into it. It gives you the map you need to navigate away from the parts that aren't working and toward the person you're actively choosing to become. That's not a small shift. Over 98 days of consistent, intentional work, it becomes the difference between someone who's reacting to an inherited script and someone who's writing their own.

The Personal Narrative Shift

You've been telling yourself a story for years. Maybe it's the story of someone who's "not a natural leader." Maybe it's the story of someone who's "always been bad with money." Maybe it's "I'm too introverted to network," or "I'm the kind of person who starts things but never finishes them," or "I've never been good at the creative stuff." These stories feel like honest self-assessments. They feel like you're just being realistic about your limitations.

They're not assessments. They're conclusions you drew at some point, often based on limited evidence, and then kept repeating until they felt like permanent facts.

The distinction matters enormously. A fact is fixed. A story can be rewritten. And the moment you understand that your personal narrative is a story, not a sentence, something opens up. You stop being a character in a plot that's already been decided and start being the person holding the pen.

Think about what happens to a story when you change one word. "I've always been bad at relationships" becomes "I've never learned how to communicate the way I want to." The first version is a verdict. The second is a gap that can be closed. "I'm not disciplined enough" becomes "I haven't built the right structure yet." The first makes discipline a personality trait you either have or don't. The second makes it a skill you can develop. The facts of your history don't change. But the meaning you assign to them, and therefore the direction they point you in, changes completely.

The Personal Narrative Shift is a four-step process. Work through it carefully, because rushing it produces surface-level results that don't stick.

Step one is to identify the story. Write down one negative narrative you carry about yourself. It should be something you've said to yourself or others more than once, something that's been functioning as an explanation for why you haven't done something or why something hasn't worked. Write it in the exact words you use internally. Not a cleaned-up version. The actual words.

Step two is to trace the origin. Ask yourself: where did this story come from? When did I first decide this was true about me? Was there a specific event, a comment someone made, a repeated pattern of failure in one area? Most limiting narratives have a specific birth point. Someone told you that you weren't creative in third grade and you filed it away as fact. You failed at something publicly once and concluded it meant something permanent about your character. You watched a parent struggle with something and assumed the struggle was hereditary. Finding the origin doesn't excuse the story or validate it. It just shows you that it was created at a specific moment in time, which means it can be changed at a specific moment in time too, specifically this one.

Step three is to challenge the evidence. Ask these questions in writing. What actual evidence supports this story? What evidence contradicts it? Have there been times when this story wasn't true? What would someone who believed the opposite story about themselves do differently than I do? That last question is especially useful. It forces you to think behaviorally rather than abstractly. You're not just questioning a belief in theory. You're identifying the specific actions the new story would produce.

Step four is to write the new story. This is your reframed narrative, written as a first-person present-tense statement. Not "someday I'll be better at this." Not "I'm trying to be more like that." Present tense. "I am someone who learns from difficulty and gets stronger because of it." "I am building the communication skills that create the relationships I want." "I am the kind of person who follows through, and I'm proving it every day." Write the new story in your journal. Then say it out loud, clearly, like you mean it. Then write it on a card and put it somewhere you'll see it every morning.

Your inner voice will push back. That's expected. The old story has years of repetition behind it. The new one has about thirty seconds. The way you close that gap is through consistent repetition of the new story, combined with consistent action that generates real evidence for it. Every time you follow through on a small commitment, you're adding a piece of evidence to the new story's case. Every time you catch yourself defaulting to the old narrative and choose to redirect, you're weakening its hold. Over time, the new story stops feeling like something you're trying to believe and starts feeling like something you simply know.

The identity map is a tool that brings all of this together visually, and it's one of the most clarifying exercises in this entire takeover. Take a blank page, physical or digital, and put your name in the center. Then draw branches outward into four categories: Roles, Values, Passions, and Qualities. Under Roles, list every significant role you currently hold, professionally and personally. Under Values, list the principles you actually live by, not the ones you think you should have. Under Passions, list the things that genuinely light you up, the activities or topics that make you lose track of time. Under Qualities, use your ten words from the first section of this chapter.

Once you've filled in all four branches, look for the connections between them. Where do your values show up in your passions? Where do your qualities express themselves in your roles? Where are there tensions, places where a role you're in conflicts with a value you hold, or where a passion is completely absent from your daily life? Those connections and tensions are the most useful information on the whole map. The connections show you where you're already living in alignment. The tensions show you where the work is.

Share the map with someone you trust and explain what it means to you. Not for their approval, but because articulating it out loud forces you to own it. There's something that shifts when you say "this is who I am" to another person. It becomes more real. It becomes harder to ignore. And in the context of a 98-day takeover built around daily action and visible progress, making your identity real and visible is exactly the kind of anchor that keeps you moving forward when the work gets hard.

The narrative you carry about yourself determines what you attempt, what you avoid, how you respond to failure, and what you believe is available to you. Changing that narrative isn't soft work. It's the most practical thing you can do, because every other change in this takeover, the habits, the leadership, the relationships, the resilience, will be filtered through the story you tell about who you are. Build a story that's honest, grounded, and genuinely yours, and everything else in these 98 days gets a better foundation to stand on.

Putting It Into Practice

Phase 3 asks you to do something most people spend their entire lives avoiding: look directly at who you actually are, separate from every role, every label, and every story you've inherited or invented. That's not comfortable. It's also not optional if you're serious about the kind of total life redesign this takeover is built around. You can't build something new on a foundation you haven't examined.

Here are four specific actions to complete before moving into Phase 4. Each one builds on the work you've done in this chapter. Don't skip them. Don't rush them. Give each one the time it actually needs.

The first action is to complete the Ten Core Qualities Exercise. Set a timer for fifteen minutes. Write twenty words that describe your true character, independent of any role or title. Narrow them down to ten. Then write two to three sentences for each word explaining how that quality shows up in your life right now and how you want to express it more fully going forward. This isn't a quick list. It's a document you'll refer back to throughout the rest of the takeover.

The second action is to complete the Inherited versus Chosen Beliefs exercise. Draw the two columns. Fill the Inherited side honestly, including the beliefs you're not proud of carrying. Mark the ones with question marks. Then write one specific belief you're consciously choosing to replace, along with the new belief you're adopting and one action you'll take this week that generates evidence for the new belief. The action has to be concrete. Not "I'll try to think differently." Something you can actually do and check off.

The third action is to write your Personal Narrative Shift. Follow all four steps: identify the story, trace its origin, challenge the evidence, and write the new story in present tense. Write the new story on a physical card. Put it somewhere you'll see it every morning this week. Read it out loud every day for the next seven days. By day seven, notice whether it's starting to feel less foreign.

The fourth action is to create your Identity Map. Use a full page. Fill in all four branches, Roles, Values, Passions, and Qualities, with real, honest answers. Circle three connections you find between different branches. Put a box around one tension you notice. Write two sentences about what that tension is telling you and what you want to do about it. Then share the map with one person and explain it to them in your own words.

These four actions together are the core of Phase 3. They're not theoretical exercises. Each one produces something tangible: a document, a belief statement, a written narrative, a visual map. Tangible things can be revisited, refined, and built upon. They hold you accountable in a way that vague intentions never can. That's the point. The 98-Day Superior Self Takeover is a system, and systems work because they produce real outputs, not just good intentions.

Who you are is not fixed. It's not finished. It's being shaped every single day by the choices you make, the stories you tell, and the actions you take. Phase 3 gives you the tools to make that shaping intentional, so that the person you're becoming is one you actually chose, not one that just happened to you by default.

Phase 4: Unlock the Secrets to Understanding

You've done serious work getting to this point. You've examined your beliefs, mapped your identity, and started to see your automatic patterns with clearer eyes. That foundation matters. Because now the work moves outward. Not just how you see yourself, but how you see everyone else around you, and how accurately you're actually doing it.

Most communication problems aren't really communication problems. They're perception problems. Two people can be in the same conversation and walk away with completely different versions of what just happened. One person feels heard. The other feels dismissed. One person thought everything was fine. The other went home frustrated. Neither one is lying. They're just seeing through different lenses, and neither one has stopped to clean theirs.

That's what this phase is about. Understanding, real understanding, not just the surface-level kind where you nod along and wait for your turn to talk. The kind that actually changes how you show up in a room, how you handle conflict, how you build trust, and how you make decisions when the answer isn't obvious. These are skills that separate people who are technically competent from people who are genuinely effective. And they're learnable. Every single one of them.

The Lens of Experience Reset

Every person you've ever met, every situation you've ever walked into, you didn't see it as it actually was. You saw it through everything you've already lived. Your past experiences, your old wounds, your previous wins and losses, all of it sits between you and reality like a filter. The filter is invisible, which is what makes it so powerful.

Think about how this actually plays out. You've had a manager who micromanaged you for two years, criticized your work in front of others, and made you feel like you couldn't do anything right. Then you get a new job. Your new manager asks to review your work before it goes out.

Logically, you know this is a different person in a different company. But something in you tightens. You feel defensive before anything has even happened. You interpret their request as distrust, even if they're just trying to support you. That reaction isn't coming from the present. It's coming from your history.

This is what psychologists call a perceptual filter, and everyone has one. It's built from years of accumulated experience, and it works fast. Before your conscious mind has time to evaluate a situation, your filter has already assigned meaning to it. That meaning feels like the truth. Often, it isn't.

Consider a hypothetical scenario: imagine someone like Tariq, a 34-year-old product manager who had grown up in a household where disagreement always escalated into conflict. Arguments at home were loud, personal, and usually ended with someone feeling hurt. By the time Tariq reached his career, he'd developed a strong aversion to any kind of pushback. When a colleague challenged his ideas in a meeting, even calmly and professionally, Tariq's body went into a mild version of the same alert it used to feel at the dinner table. He'd shut down, stop engaging, and later tell himself the colleague was just being difficult. He wasn't seeing the colleague clearly. He was seeing his childhood kitchen. Once Tariq recognized this pattern, he didn't stop feeling the discomfort, but he did stop treating it as reliable information about the person in front of him. That gap, between the feeling and the conclusion, changed everything about how he navigated disagreement at work.

Cleaning the lens doesn't mean pretending your past didn't happen. It means learning to recognize when your past is doing the interpreting for you, and pausing long enough to ask whether that interpretation is actually accurate right now.

Here's how to do this in practice. At the end of each day this week, pick one interaction that felt charged, uncomfortable, or confusing. Write down what happened in one or two sentences. Then ask yourself three specific questions. First: what did I feel during this interaction and where in my body did I feel it? Second: what meaning did I assign to the other person's behavior? Third: is there any way my past history might be coloring that meaning? You're not trying to excuse the other person or dismiss your feelings. You're trying to separate what actually happened from the story your filter added on top of it.

Over time, this practice builds something genuinely valuable: the ability to see people as they are rather than as your history has prepared you to see them. That's not just useful for your relationships. It's useful for every decision you make that involves another person, which is most of them.

Your past is a lens. You get to decide how clean it is.

Listening to Understand vs. Replying

Most people aren't listening. They're waiting.

While someone else is talking, there's a parallel process running in most people's heads. They're evaluating what's being said, forming a response, deciding whether they agree, thinking about a related story they want to share, or mentally drafting a counterargument. The other person's words are still coming in, but they're being processed through the filter of "how do I respond to this?" rather than "what is this person actually trying to say?"

That's not listening. That's preparation for speaking.

Real listening, the kind that actually builds trust and uncovers what people mean rather than just what they say, requires something most people find genuinely difficult: silence. Not the silence of waiting for your turn. The silence of being fully present with someone else's experience without rushing to evaluate it, fix it, or respond to it.

The difference in outcome is significant. When people feel truly heard, they open up. They share more. They trust more. They're more willing to be honest about what's actually going on. When they feel like they're talking to someone who's already composing a response, they sense it, and they pull back. They give you the surface version. They stop trying to explain the real thing because they don't feel like you're actually there to receive it.

Think about a hypothetical scenario: imagine someone like Jasmine, a 31-year-old team lead who prided herself on being a good communicator. She was articulate, quick-thinking, and always had a thoughtful response ready. But her team kept telling her in anonymous feedback surveys that they didn't feel comfortable bringing her problems. She was confused. She was available. She responded quickly. She gave good advice. What she didn't realize was that she was so focused on having the right answer that she never let anyone finish explaining the actual problem. She'd identify the issue partway through and pivot to solutions before the other person had finished speaking. Her team didn't need better answers from her. They needed to feel like she was actually with them. When Jasmine started practicing full, silent listening, where she committed to not speaking until the other person had completely finished and there was a natural pause, the feedback shifted within weeks. People started coming to her more, not less. She was giving them the same amount of time. She was just using it differently.

The practice is called focused listening, and it has four specific components. First, make a physical commitment to the conversation. Put your phone face down or out of reach. Turn your body toward the person. Make steady, natural eye contact. These physical signals tell the other person, before a word is spoken, that you're actually present.

Second, listen for what's underneath the words. People rarely say exactly what they mean on the first try. They circle around it. They test whether it's safe to say the real thing. Pay attention to tone, to the words they repeat, to what they seem to be reaching for but can't quite articulate. The most important thing someone is trying to tell you is often just below the surface of what they're actually saying.

Third, don't fill the silence. When someone finishes speaking, most people jump in within one or two seconds. Try waiting three to five seconds before responding. That pause does two things. It signals that you're actually thinking about what they said rather than just reacting. And it often prompts the other person to add something they were holding back, something more honest or more specific than what they said first.

Fourth, reflect before you respond. Before you share your view, your solution, or your related experience, say back what you heard in your own words. Not a word-for-word repeat. A genuine summary: "So if I'm understanding you right, what's really frustrating isn't the deadline itself, it's feeling like you didn't have enough input into setting it. Is that right?" That one step alone prevents more misunderstandings than almost any other communication practice.

Understanding grows in the space between words. It lives in the pause where you stop trying to be heard and start truly hearing. The deepest connections aren't built on what you say. They're built on what you choose to understand.

Challenging Invisible Assumptions

Your brain makes thousands of micro-decisions every day, and most of them are shortcuts. When you meet someone new, your brain scans for patterns and generates an instant assessment. When a colleague sends a short, clipped email, you decide what it means. When a meeting gets canceled without explanation, you fill in the reason. When someone doesn't respond to your message, you draw a conclusion. These mental shortcuts happen in milliseconds, and they feel like perception. They're not. They're guesses dressed up as facts.

The problem isn't that you make assumptions. That's unavoidable. The human brain is a pattern-recognition machine, and shortcuts are how it keeps you from being overwhelmed by information. The problem is when you stop treating your assumptions as guesses and start treating them as certainties. That's when they close doors.

A colleague who seems cold might be going through something at home. A client who pushes back hard might actually be your biggest champion once they feel heard. A team member who's been quiet in meetings might have the most valuable perspective in the room. Every one of these situations can go one of two ways depending on whether you approach it with a conclusion already formed or with a question still open.

The single most useful question you can ask when you feel certain about someone or something is this: "What else could be true?"

It sounds simple. It's not always easy. When you're frustrated, when you feel disrespected, when something hasn't gone the way you expected, your brain wants a clean explanation. It wants to assign blame, identify the problem, and move on. "What else could be true?" interrupts that process. It forces your brain to hold the situation open a little longer, to consider that your first read might be incomplete.

Here's how to build this into your daily life in a concrete way. Keep a small note in your phone or journal called "Assumptions I'm Testing." When you notice yourself making a judgment about a person or situation, especially a negative one, write it down. Then write at least two alternative explanations that could also be true. You don't have to believe the alternatives. You just have to write them. That act alone creates enough mental distance from your original conclusion to stop it from running unchecked.

The next step is to gather real information. This means asking a direct, non-confrontational question rather than acting on your assumption. "I noticed you seemed quieter than usual in the meeting today. Is everything okay?" "I got the sense that my proposal missed something for you. Can you tell me more about what you're looking for?" These questions aren't weakness. They're precision. They replace guesswork with actual data, and actual data leads to better decisions.

Assumptions can close doors. Curiosity opens them. That's not just a nice idea. It's a practical operating principle. The professionals who are most effective at building relationships, resolving conflicts, and creating collaboration aren't the ones with the best answers. They're the ones who ask the best questions.

The quality of your questions shapes the quality of your outcomes. Ask better questions and you'll uncover better information. Ask deeper questions and you'll find what's actually going on beneath the surface. The next time you feel stuck in a conflict or a misunderstanding, don't push harder with your current interpretation. Ask a better question instead.

There's something deeply uncomfortable about not knowing. The brain doesn't like open loops. It doesn't like unresolved situations, ambiguous people, or problems without clear answers. So it does what it's built to do: it closes the loop as fast as possible. It picks an explanation, assigns a label, and moves on. Problem solved.

Except the problem usually isn't solved. It's just been simplified beyond recognition.

Most of the situations that actually matter in your professional and personal life aren't simple. They're layered. A team member's performance issues might be about skills, or personal circumstances, or management style, or all three at once. A business decision that looks clear on paper might have implications that don't show up for six months. A relationship that feels like it's going wrong might just be going through a transition. When you rush to a conclusion because uncertainty is uncomfortable, you often solve the wrong problem, or you solve the right problem in the wrong way, because you didn't give yourself enough time to actually understand it.

Sitting with uncertainty is a skill. It doesn't come naturally to most high-achieving people, because high achievers are wired for action and resolution. Waiting feels like losing. Not having an answer feels like falling behind. But the ability to stay in a complex situation without forcing a premature conclusion is one of the most valuable capabilities you can develop, both as a leader and as a person.

Think about a hypothetical scenario: imagine someone like Camille, a 39-year-old operations director who was known for her decisiveness. She was fast, she was clear, and she got things done. But she kept running into the same pattern: she'd make a call on a complex situation, implement it quickly, and then find herself backtracking two weeks later when information she hadn't waited for came to light. The speed she thought was a strength was actually costing her more time than it saved. When she started practicing what she called "intentional pause," giving herself a defined window of time before deciding on anything with significant stakes, the quality of her decisions improved noticeably. Not because she became slower. Because she became more accurate.

Here's a specific practice for building comfort with uncertainty. When you face a complex problem or an unclear situation, write it down at the top of a blank page. Then write three things you know for certain about it. Then write three things you don't know yet. Then write one question you could ask or one piece of information you could gather that would reduce the uncertainty meaningfully. That's your next action. Not a full solution. Just the next right question.

This practice does something important. It separates what you actually know from what you're assuming, which is the same work you did in the previous section, applied now to complex situations rather than individual people. And it gives you a concrete next step that moves you toward clarity without forcing you to pretend you have answers you don't have yet.

Saying "I don't know" is not a sign of weakness. For most professionals, it feels like one, which is why so few people say it. But the willingness to say "I don't know yet, and I want to find out" signals intellectual honesty, and intellectual honesty builds more trust than false certainty ever does. The people around you already know when you're guessing. When you pretend otherwise, you don't fool them. You just lose credibility.

Real growth doesn't happen in the clean, certain, comfortable parts of your life. It happens in the gray areas, the situations where the answer isn't obvious, where the right path isn't clear, where you have to hold multiple possibilities at once and keep moving anyway. That's where you find out what you're actually made of. And that's where the most meaningful decisions get made.

You don't have to figure everything out right now. Sometimes understanding means staying in the question long enough for the real answer to show up.

Phase 4 has covered a lot of ground, and the through-line across all of it is this: understanding is an active practice, not a passive state. You don't arrive at it by waiting. You build it through specific, repeated behaviors. Cleaning your perceptual lens. Listening without preparing your response. Questioning your assumptions before acting on them. Staying in complexity long enough to actually understand it. These four skills work together. They reinforce each other. And they compound over time in the same way every other skill in this takeover does.

Curiosity and empathy are the tools that hold all of this together. Curiosity asks better questions. Empathy creates the conditions where honest answers can actually come. Together, they're what turn surface-level interactions into real connection, and real connection is what makes everything else in your professional and personal life work better.

Here are three specific actions to complete before you move into Phase 5.

The first action: in your next meeting or significant conversation, commit to listening without planning your response. Before the conversation starts, write this at the top of your notes: "Listen first. Understand before responding." When the other person is speaking, keep your pen down. Don't formulate your reply. Just take in what they're saying. After they finish, wait three full seconds before you speak. Then, before you share your own view, reflect back what you heard in one or two sentences and ask if you got it right. Do this once and notice how the quality of the conversation shifts.

The second action: identify one assumption you currently hold about a colleague, a client, or someone in your personal life. Write it down exactly as it sounds in your head. Then write two alternative explanations that could also be true. Then identify one specific question you could ask that would give you real information rather than leaving you working from guesswork. Ask that question this week. Write down what you learn. You'll almost certainly find that the real situation is more nuanced than your original assumption allowed for.

The third action: the next time you face a situation where you feel pressure to have an answer you don't actually have, practice saying "I don't know yet, but I want to find out." Say it clearly, without apology. Then use the three-part uncertainty practice from this chapter: write what you know, write what you don't know, and identify the one question that would move you toward clarity. Work that question before you work the solution. The answer you find will be better for it.

Every conversation you have from this point forward is an opportunity to practice what this phase has taught you. Every charged interaction is a chance to check your lens. Every moment of uncertainty is a chance to stay curious instead of rushing to close. These aren't abstract ideals. They're daily choices, and the 98-Day Superior Self Takeover is built on the truth that daily choices, made consistently, become the person you are.

Phase 5: Core Values and Decision Making

Identifying Your Non-Negotiables

You've spent the last four phases learning to see yourself more clearly. You've examined your beliefs, mapped your identity, and started to understand how your past shapes the way you interpret the present. All of that work was pointing toward something. It was pointing here, to the question that sits at the center of every meaningful decision you'll ever make: what do you actually stand for?

Most people have never answered that question with any real precision. They have a general sense of what they think is good. They believe in being honest, working hard, treating people well. But vague ideas about goodness aren't the same as a clear set of personal values. And the difference between the two shows up every single time you face a hard choice, a high-stakes decision, or a situation where two things you care about are pulling in opposite directions. Without a specific, ranked list of what matters most to you, you make those decisions based on whatever feels right in the moment. That's not a strategy. That's a coin flip dressed up as judgment.

Your core values are the principles that guide how you live. They're the beliefs that shape your decisions, your actions, and your character. When you live in line with your values, something settles inside you. You feel grounded. You feel like yourself. When you act against your values, even when no one else knows it, there's a friction you can't quite shake. A low-level unease. A sense that something's off. That feeling isn't random. It's information, and it's telling you that your actions and your principles aren't matching up.

The goal of this section is to take you from a vague sense of what you care about to a specific, written list of your top five non-negotiables. These are the values that are so central to who you are that compromising them costs you something real. Not just discomfort. Something that erodes your sense of integrity over time.

The most reliable way to identify your true values isn't to sit down and think about what sounds good. It's to look at your actual lived experience and let it tell you. Start by thinking about three or four moments in your life when you felt genuinely proud, energized, or deeply fulfilled. Not just happy, but aligned. Like you were doing exactly what you were supposed to be doing, in exactly the way you were supposed to do it. Write those moments down. Then ask yourself: what was happening in each one? What were you doing? Who were you with? What principles were you living out in those moments?

Now do the opposite. Think about two or three moments when you felt drained, resentful, or genuinely conflicted. Times when you went along with something that didn't sit right with you, or when you stayed in a situation that felt wrong but you couldn't explain why. Write those down too. Then ask: what was being violated in those moments? What did you feel you were being asked to betray? The answer to that question points directly at a value you hold deeply, often more clearly than the positive moments do, because the pain of a violated value is much harder to ignore than the quiet satisfaction of an honored one.

Consider a hypothetical scenario: imagine someone like Nadia, a 33-year-old account manager at a consulting firm. She was good at her job and well-liked by her team. But she'd been feeling a creeping resentment for about a year that she couldn't fully explain. She wasn't burned out exactly. She still had energy. She just felt hollow. When she went through this reflection process, the pattern became clear fast. Her proudest moments had all involved being completely honest with clients, even when the truth was uncomfortable. Her most draining moments had all involved being asked to soften data, spin results, or frame things in ways that weren't fully accurate. Integrity wasn't just something she valued in theory. It was a non-negotiable for her. The moment she named it clearly, she understood exactly why the past year had felt so corrosive. She hadn't been living in line with one of her most fundamental principles, and her nervous system had been registering that gap every single day.

Once you've done the reflection work, you'll likely have a long and somewhat messy list of things that matter to you. That's normal. The next step is to narrow it down. Look at your list and start grouping things that are related. "Honesty" and "transparency" are probably the same value. "Growth" and "learning" might be one thing. "Family" and "connection" might point toward the same underlying principle. Start collapsing the list until you have somewhere between eight and twelve distinct values.

Then comes the harder part.

You need to rank them. Not because some values are objectively more important than others, but because when two of your values conflict, and they will, you need to know which one wins. If you value both freedom and security, and a decision forces you to choose between them, which one do you protect? If you value both loyalty and honesty, and being honest with someone would feel disloyal to another person, where do you land? Without a ranking, you're back to making it up in the moment. With a ranking, you have a compass.

Here's the specific process for ranking. Take your list of eight to twelve values and ask yourself this question about each pair: if I could only honor one of these two values in a given situation, which one would I choose? Work through the list systematically, comparing each value to every other one. It's slow, but it's worth it. By the end, the order will become clear. Your top five will rise to the surface not because they sound the best, but because when you actually test them against each other, they consistently win.

Write your top five on a clean page. These are your non-negotiables. They're the principles you will not compromise on, regardless of the pressure, the incentive, or the convenience. Protect them. Not because someone told you to, but because you now know exactly what it costs you when you don't.

Every major decision you face from this point forward gets filtered through this list. Before you accept a job, ask whether the role will let you live by your top values. Before you commit to a relationship or a partnership, ask whether this person respects the principles you've just named. Before you agree to something that feels wrong, ask which value is being violated and whether the trade-off is actually worth it. This is what it means to use your values as a compass. Not as a rigid rule book, but as a reliable reference point that cuts through the noise when the stakes are high.

Your values aren't just abstract ideals. They're practical tools. And now you know exactly what yours are.

Resolving Values Conflicts

Knowing your values is one thing. Living by them when the pressure is on is something else entirely.

Values conflicts are inevitable. They show up in your career when your company asks you to do something that sits uncomfortably against your principles. They show up in relationships when the people you love want things that pull against what you believe in. They show up in your own head when two things you care about deeply are pointing in completely different directions. Most people handle these conflicts by suppressing one value in favor of the other without consciously choosing to do so. They just go along with whatever path has the least immediate friction. And then they wonder why they feel resentful, depleted, or quietly dissatisfied even when things look fine from the outside.

That quiet dissatisfaction has a name. It's called values misalignment, and it's one of the most common and least talked-about sources of burnout among high-achieving professionals. You can work hard, hit your targets, earn good money, and still feel hollow if the way you're spending your time and energy doesn't reflect what you actually believe in. The exhaustion isn't from the work itself. It's from the constant, low-level cost of acting against your own principles day after day.

Think about a hypothetical scenario: imagine someone like Jerome, a 36-year-old sales director at a tech company. He was hitting his numbers. His team liked him. By every external measure, he was succeeding. But he'd been waking up at 3 a.m. a few times a week with a vague, unspecified dread. He couldn't pin it down. When he worked through his values, he identified that integrity and genuine service to clients were two of his top three principles. Then he looked at what his daily work actually required. He was being pushed to close deals quickly, sometimes before clients were fully ready, using urgency tactics that he knew created buyer's remorse. He was hitting his numbers by doing things that violated his core principles. The 3 a.m. wake-ups weren't anxiety. They were his values trying to get his attention. Once he saw the conflict clearly, he had a real decision to make, and for the first time, he was making it consciously instead of just drifting through it.

The first step in resolving any values conflict is to name it precisely. Not "I feel off about this" or "something doesn't feel right." Name the specific values on each side of the tension. "I value loyalty to my team AND I value honesty with my leadership, and right now those two things are asking me to do opposite things." Getting that specific changes everything. You stop feeling a vague discomfort and start seeing a clear problem with a real structure. And problems with clear structures can be solved.

Once you've named the conflict, the second step is to understand what's actually driving it. Ask yourself three questions. Is this conflict based on a misunderstanding that better communication could resolve? Is it based on a lack of clarity about what's actually being asked of me? Or is it a genuine clash of principles where two things I care about are fundamentally incompatible in this situation? The answer determines your path forward. A misunderstanding calls for a conversation. A lack of clarity calls for more information. A genuine clash of principles calls for a decision.

For the conflicts that require a decision, go back to your ranked list of non-negotiables. Which value sits higher? That's your answer. Not comfortable, necessarily. But clear. And clear is what you need when the stakes are real.

The third step is to take action that reflects your decision. This is where most people stall. They identify the conflict, they know what their values say, and then they do nothing because the action required is difficult or uncertain. But inaction is also a choice. Staying in a situation that violates your values, without doing anything to change it, is a choice to keep paying the cost. The action you take doesn't have to be dramatic. It might be a direct conversation where you explain what you need. It might be a boundary you set clearly and calmly. It might be a decision to leave a role, a relationship, or a commitment that can't be made compatible with who you are. The scale of the action matters less than the fact that you're taking it consciously, based on your principles, rather than just reacting or avoiding.

Boundaries are one of the most practical tools for protecting your values in daily life. A boundary isn't a wall and it isn't an ultimatum. It's a clear statement of what you will and won't do, based on what you believe in. Setting a boundary that's rooted in a core value feels completely different from setting one based on preference or mood. It's grounded. It's calm. And it's much easier to hold because you know exactly why it exists.

Think about the difference between saying "I don't want to take on that project" and saying "I can't take on that project in a way that meets the standard I hold for my work, given my current commitments, and I'm not willing to do it badly." The second statement is a values-based boundary. It's honest, it's specific, and it's hard to argue with because it's not about preference. It's about integrity.

Communication is the other critical tool for resolving values conflicts, especially in relationships. A lot of the tension that builds between people isn't because their values are incompatible. It's because they've never actually named their values to each other. They've been operating on assumptions about what the other person believes and wants. When you can say clearly and calmly, "this matters to me because of this specific principle," you give the other person something real to work with. They can disagree with your position, but they can't dismiss the fact that you have a principled reason for it. That changes the nature of the conversation entirely.

A values conflict that you ignore doesn't resolve itself. It compounds. What starts as a quiet friction becomes a steady resentment. What starts as a small compromise becomes a pattern of compromising. The people who feel most burned out, most disconnected from their work, most hollow in their relationships, are almost always people who've been making small, unexamined compromises against their core principles for a long time. The solution isn't to wait until the resentment becomes unbearable. The solution is to catch the conflict early, name it clearly, and address it while it's still manageable.

Your values don't change every time the situation changes. That's what makes them values rather than preferences. But the way you express and protect them will look different in different contexts. The skill you're building here isn't rigidity. It's discernment. Knowing when to hold firm, when to have the conversation, when to set the boundary, and when to make the hard call. That discernment, grounded in a clear set of principles, is what turns good intentions into actual integrity.

Every choice you make is a vote for the person you want to be. When you make choices that honor your non-negotiables, you build a track record of integrity with yourself. That track record is what real confidence is built on. Not the confidence that comes from external validation or a good performance review, but the quiet, steady confidence that comes from knowing you've been true to what you believe in, even when it was inconvenient.

Your Next Move

Phase 5 has been about one thing at its core: closing the gap between what you believe and how you live. That gap is where stress lives. Where resentment grows. Where the version of yourself you're trying to build keeps getting undermined by choices that don't reflect your actual principles. The work you've done in this chapter gives you the tools to close that gap deliberately, one decision at a time.

The 98-Day Superior Self Takeover is a system built on daily, intentional action. Phase 5 is no different. The insights you've gained here only become real when you put them to work in your actual life today, not eventually, not when things calm down. Today.

Here are three specific actions to complete before you move into Phase 6. Each one is concrete, doable, and designed to produce something you can build on.

The first action is to complete your values ranking. If you haven't done the full reflection process yet, do it now. Write down your peak moments and your most draining moments. Extract the values from each. Group and collapse your list down to eight to twelve distinct principles. Then do the head-to-head comparison process until your top five rise to the surface. Write them in order on a clean page, number one through five. Label this page "My Non-Negotiables" and put it somewhere you'll see it regularly. Your journal, your desk, the notes app on your phone. This isn't a one-time exercise. It's a reference document you'll use for every significant decision you face from here on.

The second action is to identify one area in your current life where your daily actions are in conflict with one of your top five values. Be specific. Not "I feel like work doesn't align with my values." Name the exact value. Name the exact behavior or situation that's violating it. Write one sentence describing the conflict clearly. Then write one concrete action you can take within the next 48 hours to begin addressing it. That action might be a conversation you need to have. A boundary you need to set. A commitment you need to walk back. A decision you've been avoiding. Whatever it is, write it down and schedule it. Give it a specific time and day. Vague intentions don't survive contact with a busy week. Scheduled actions do.

The third action is the simplest and the most immediate. Today, before this day ends, make one deliberate choice based solely on your top value. It doesn't have to be a big choice. It can be small. Decline a meeting that consistently wastes your time because you value focused, meaningful work. Say something honest in a conversation where you'd normally soften the truth because you value integrity. Protect an hour of your evening for something that matters to you because you value your own wellbeing. The size of the choice isn't the point. The point is that you make it consciously, with your top value as the only filter. Then write down what you chose and how it felt to make that choice from that place. That record becomes the first entry in your values-in-action log, proof that living by your principles isn't a theory. It's something you're already doing.

Phase 6: Discovering and Fueling Your True Passion

You've done the hard internal work. You've examined your beliefs, mapped your identity, cleaned your perceptual lens, and named your core values. That work wasn't preparation for something easier. It was preparation for something deeper. Because now the question shifts from "who am I?" to "what actually lights me up?" And for a lot of working professionals and entrepreneurs, that question is surprisingly difficult to answer.

Not because the answer doesn't exist. It does. It's just been buried under years of practicality, obligation, and the quiet habit of putting what's responsible ahead of what's real.

Passion gets talked about in ways that make it sound like a lightning bolt. Like one day you'll be sitting at your desk and suddenly you'll know, with complete certainty, exactly what you're meant to do with your life. That almost never happens. For most people, passion isn't a moment. It's a direction. It shows up slowly, in the things you keep coming back to, in the topics you can talk about for hours without noticing the time, in the work that doesn't feel like work even when it's hard. Finding it requires looking carefully at what's already there, not waiting for something dramatic to arrive.

That's what this phase is about. Not inventing a passion from scratch. Uncovering the one that's already been trying to get your attention.

The Search for Passion

There's a specific reason passion feels hard to find for so many driven, capable people. It's not that they lack depth or curiosity. It's that they've spent years being rewarded for competence, not for enthusiasm. They got promoted because they were good at the job, not because the job lit them up. They chose their career path based on what made sense, what paid well, what their family expected, or what they happened to be skilled at early on. Passion, if it was considered at all, was treated as a bonus. Something nice to have if it happened to align with the practical choice. Not something worth actively searching for.

The cost of that approach compounds quietly over time. You can be successful by every external measure and still feel like something essential is missing. That's not ingratitude. That's the gap between competence and passion showing up in your daily experience.

The good news is that passion isn't a fixed trait. You don't either have it or you don't. It's something that gets activated through engagement, through curiosity, through paying attention to what genuinely moves you rather than what you're supposed to care about. And the search for it starts with a very specific kind of self-examination.

Think about a hypothetical scenario: imagine someone like Marcus, a 34-year-old financial analyst who was objectively excellent at his work. He was precise, methodical, and highly regarded by his firm. But every Sunday evening he felt a dull weight he couldn't name. He'd tried to dismiss it as stress or burnout. When he actually sat down and traced it, he realized he hadn't felt genuinely excited about his work in over four years. He'd been coasting on competence. When he looked back at the moments in his career where he'd felt most alive, they weren't the moments he'd closed the biggest deals. They were the moments he'd explained complex financial concepts to junior team members in a way that finally clicked for them. He loved teaching. He loved breaking things down. He'd just never paid attention to that pattern because it wasn't his official job description. That one observation, pulled from his own history, became the thread he started following.

That's how the search works. You look at your own life, your own history, your own patterns of engagement, and you let them tell you something.

Start with the Flow Inventory. This is a structured reflection exercise that takes about twenty minutes and produces real, usable information. Open your journal or a blank document and write down every activity, topic, or type of work that has ever caused you to lose track of time. Go back as far as you can. Include things from childhood, from school, from hobbies, from side projects, from conversations you've had. Don't filter for practicality. Don't ask whether it could ever make money or whether it fits your current life. Just write what genuinely absorbs you when you're in it.

Once you have that list, look for the patterns. Are there themes that keep appearing? Skills that show up across different activities? Types of problems you're drawn to solving? Types of people you love being around when you're doing your best work? The pattern underneath the specific activities is where your passion lives. It's rarely about the exact thing. It's about what the thing gives you: a sense of impact, a feeling of creative flow, the satisfaction of solving something complex, the energy of connecting with others. Name the pattern, not just the activity.

The second part of the search involves your strengths, and this is where a lot of people make a critical mistake. They confuse what they're good at with what they love. These two things overlap sometimes, but not always. You might be excellent at writing reports and find it completely draining. You might be a natural at public speaking but never get asked to do it. The intersection you're looking for isn't just where your interests live or just where your strengths live. It's the specific place where both show up at the same time. That intersection is where passion becomes sustainable, because it's grounded in both energy and capability.

To find that intersection, take your Flow Inventory list and put it next to the list of your ten core qualities from Phase 3. Look for the activities on your flow list that also draw on your deepest qualities. If "curiosity" is one of your core qualities, which activities on your flow list require and reward curiosity? If "connecting with people" is one of your qualities, which activities on your list involve meaningful human interaction? Where those two lists overlap is the beginning of your answer.

Fear is the other major factor in this section, and it deserves to be named directly. For a lot of people, the reason they haven't pursued what actually excites them isn't that they don't know what it is. It's that they do know, and it scares them. Pursuing something you genuinely care about feels far more vulnerable than pursuing something you're simply good at. If you fail at a job you were never that invested in, it stings but it doesn't cut deep. If you fail at something that actually matters to you, that feels like a verdict on who you are. So the safer move, the one most people make without fully realizing it, is to never fully commit. To keep the passion at arm's length. To stay in the competence zone where the stakes feel lower.

That protection comes at a cost. The cost is the hollow feeling Marcus was carrying every Sunday evening. The cost is a life that looks successful from the outside and feels like going through the motions from the inside. Naming the fear doesn't eliminate it. But it does strip it of some of its power. When you can say clearly "I'm afraid that if I actually pursue this, I'll find out I'm not good enough at it," you've turned a vague, paralyzing dread into a specific, addressable concern. Specific concerns can be worked with. Vague dread just runs in the background and wins by default.

Write down the one fear that's been holding you back from a passion you already know about. Not a paragraph. One sentence. "I'm afraid that if I try to write seriously, I'll find out I have nothing worth saying." "I'm afraid that if I change careers to something I love, I'll lose the financial stability I've worked hard to build." "I'm afraid that people who know me professionally will think I'm being naive or unrealistic." Get it out of your head and onto paper. Give it a name. A named fear is a fear you can actually deal with. An unnamed one just quietly runs the show.

Passion also has a relationship with purpose that's worth understanding clearly. Purpose is the broader "why" behind what you do. Passion is the fuel that keeps you moving toward it. You can have a sense of purpose without passion, but it tends to be exhausting, driven by willpower alone. You can have passion without purpose, but it tends to feel scattered, exciting in the moment but hard to sustain over time. When the two connect, when what you love doing also connects to something that feels meaningful and larger than yourself, that's when the energy becomes genuinely self-sustaining. That's the combination this phase is helping you build toward.

The search for passion isn't a one-afternoon exercise. It's an ongoing practice of paying attention. But it does start with specific actions, and those actions start right now, with what you already know about yourself from the work you've done in the previous five phases. You have more information about who you are than you did when you started. Use it.

Taking Passionate Action

Knowing what you're passionate about and actually doing something with that knowledge are two very different things. Most people get stuck in the gap between them. They identify something that genuinely excites them, they feel a brief surge of energy, and then they look at their actual life, the job, the mortgage, the family obligations, the packed schedule, and they conclude that pursuing this thing would require blowing everything up. So they don't. They file it away under "someday" and go back to what's manageable.

The problem with that logic is that "someday" almost never comes. Life doesn't clear a path. You have to carve one. And the way you carve it isn't by quitting your job and betting everything on an untested idea. It's by taking small, deliberate actions that bring your passion into your current life without requiring you to dismantle the stability you've built.

That's the core principle of this section. You're not choosing between your passion and your life. You're finding the places where passion can start to live inside the life you already have.

Think about a hypothetical scenario: imagine someone like Priya, a 31-year-old HR manager who had always loved graphic design. She'd studied it briefly before switching to a more "practical" degree. She still spent her weekends sketching layouts and playing with design software, but she'd always treated it as a hobby, something she did in her spare time that had nothing to do with her real career. When she started this phase of the takeover, she didn't quit her job. She did something much smaller. She offered to redesign the internal newsletter at work. It took her four hours on a Saturday. Her manager loved it. Three months later, she was leading the visual communication for a company-wide initiative, doing work that genuinely energized her, inside the same job she'd been in for two years. She didn't change her life. She changed how she showed up in it. That's what micro-actions do over time.

A micro-action is a small, specific step you can take today that moves you toward your passion without requiring a massive commitment of time, money, or courage. The word "micro" matters. It's not about grand gestures. It's about consistent, daily movement in the direction of what lights you up. Small actions, done regularly, create momentum. Momentum creates options. Options create real change.

The first micro-action practice is called the 15-Minute Passion Block. Pick one activity from your Flow Inventory, something that genuinely absorbs you, and commit to spending exactly fifteen minutes on it today. Not an hour. Not a whole morning. Fifteen minutes. Set a timer. Do the thing. Then stop. This matters for two reasons. First, fifteen minutes is small enough that it removes the excuse of not having time. Everyone has fifteen minutes. Second, fifteen minutes is often enough to remind your nervous system what it feels like to be genuinely engaged. That feeling is data. It tells you whether the activity is actually a source of energy or just something you think you should care about.

Do this for seven consecutive days with the same activity. By day seven, you'll know something important: whether this is a real source of passion for you or just an interesting idea. Real passion shows up consistently. It pulls you back. It makes the fifteen minutes feel too short.

If you're fighting yourself to show up for it after seven days, it might not be the right thread to pull. That's useful information too.

The second practice is what's called Passion Integration, which means finding ways to bring what you love into what you already do. This is different from carving out separate time for a passion project. It's about looking at your current role, your current relationships, your current daily life, and asking: where could more of what I love actually fit here? Priya's newsletter redesign is a good example. She didn't create a new context. She brought her passion into an existing one.

Here's how to do this specifically. Look at your current job or primary daily responsibilities. Write down the three tasks or activities you spend the most time on. Then look at your passion, the theme or intersection you identified in the previous section. Ask yourself: is there any version of these three tasks that could involve more of what I love? Could a meeting you run regularly be structured differently to involve more of your natural strengths? Could a project you're working on be approached in a way that draws on your passion? Could you volunteer for something adjacent to your role that brings you closer to what energizes you? You're not looking for a perfect overlap. You're looking for any overlap, any small entry point where passion can start to touch your daily work.

Even a ten percent increase in how much of your day involves something you genuinely care about changes how the whole day feels. That's not a small thing. Over weeks and months, it becomes significant.

The third practice is building what you might call a Passion Environment. The people around you, the content you consume, the spaces you spend time in, all of it either supports your passion or quietly works against it. If you're trying to develop a writing practice and everyone in your immediate circle treats creative work as impractical, you're swimming against a current every single day. If you're trying to build a business around something you love and you have no connection to anyone who's done something similar, you're navigating without a map.

This doesn't mean you need to find a whole new social circle. It means being intentional about adding at least one or two inputs to your environment that support what you're building. Find one online community of people who share your passion. Read one book by someone who built a life around something similar to what excites you. Reach out to one person in your existing network who seems to be living closer to their passion than you are and ask them one specific question about how they got there. These aren't dramatic changes. They're small additions to your environment that shift the ambient message from "this is impractical" to "this is possible."

There's also the matter of protecting the time and energy you're starting to dedicate to your passion. As you begin to take these micro-actions, you'll notice something: other things will try to fill that space. Requests that feel urgent. Obligations that feel unavoidable. The pull of what's familiar and comfortable. This is where the boundary work from Phase 5 becomes directly relevant. Protecting fifteen minutes a day for something that matters to you is a values-based boundary. It's not selfish. It's necessary. You can't build anything meaningful with the time left over after everything else has taken what it wants.

Say no to one low-priority obligation this week. Not to be difficult. To protect the space you're creating for something that actually matters. Notice how it feels to make that trade deliberately, to choose your passion over someone else's convenience. That feeling, even if it's a little uncomfortable at first, is the feeling of living in alignment with what you've said matters to you.

Passion also needs to be protected from your own inner critic, which will have opinions about all of this. It will tell you that you're being unrealistic. That you're too old, too busy, too far behind to start something new. That people with real responsibilities don't have the luxury of chasing what excites them. These thoughts are familiar by now. You've worked with them in Phase 1 and Phase 2. Apply the same tools here. Name the thought. Question it. Replace it with something more accurate. "I'm too old to start this" becomes "I'm starting now with everything I already know, and that's a significant advantage." "This is unrealistic" becomes "I'm testing this in small ways to find out what's actually possible."

The inner critic is loudest when you're closest to something that genuinely matters. That's not a coincidence. It's a signal worth paying attention to, just not in the way the critic intends. The louder it gets, the more likely it is that you're moving in a direction that's real for you. Keep moving.

Passion isn't a destination you arrive at and then stay in forever. It's something you have to keep feeding. The micro-actions you take today build the habit of engagement. The habit of engagement builds the evidence that this matters to you. The evidence builds the confidence to take slightly bigger steps. And those slightly bigger steps, over the course of this 98-day takeover and beyond, add up to a life that actually reflects what you care about rather than just what you've been doing by default.

You don't have to have it all figured out. You just have to take the next small step. Then the one after that. The path doesn't appear all at once. It appears one step at a time, as you walk it.

Putting It Into Practice

Passion is the fuel that makes the rest of this takeover sustainable. The habits, the leadership, the resilience, the purpose work that comes in the phases ahead, all of it gets harder to sustain when you're running on obligation alone. When what you're doing connects to something you actually care about, you show up differently. You push through resistance more readily. You recover from setbacks faster. You stay in the work longer. That's not motivation in the abstract. That's what passion actually does at a practical level.

The three actions below are designed to move you from reading about passion to actively engaging with it today. Each one is specific, concrete, and takes less time than you think.

The first action is to complete the Flow Inventory right now. Open your journal or a blank document. Set a timer for fifteen minutes. Write down every activity, topic, or type of work that has ever caused you to lose track of time. Go back as far as you need to. Don't filter for practicality. When the timer goes off, look at your list and circle the three items that feel most alive to you right now, not the most impressive ones, the most alive ones. Those three are your starting threads. Keep this list. You'll come back to it.

The second action is to dedicate fifteen minutes today, before this day ends, to one of the three circled items. Not tomorrow. Today. Set the timer. Do the thing. When it's done, write two sentences about how it felt to spend that time. Did it pull you in or did you have to push yourself through it? That answer is important information. Repeat this for the next six days with the same activity. By the end of the week you'll have something real to work with.

The third action is to identify the one fear that's been standing between you and a passion you already know about, and write it down in a single, specific sentence. Don't describe it vaguely. Name it precisely. Then write one sentence directly beneath it that challenges it. Not a pep talk. A realistic counter-statement grounded in what's actually true. "I'm afraid I'm not talented enough" becomes "I don't yet know what I'm capable of because I haven't given this consistent effort." That reframe is your working belief for the next seven days. Read it every morning before you start your day.

These three actions together take about forty minutes. They won't transform everything overnight. They're not supposed to. They're the beginning of a daily practice of paying attention to what matters and making small, deliberate moves toward it. That practice, sustained across the remaining weeks of this takeover, is what turns a dormant interest into a genuine source of energy and direction in your life.

Phase 7: Security in the Sense of Self

There's a version of confidence that most people are chasing without realizing it. It's the kind that depends on other people. On a compliment from a manager. On likes on a post. On being included in the right meeting. On getting the promotion, the approval, the nod. It feels like confidence when it's there. But the moment the validation stops, so does the feeling. That's not confidence. That's dependency with better branding.

Real security in yourself doesn't work that way. It doesn't need to be refueled by someone else's opinion every few days. It's not something you earn through achievement and lose when you fail. It's an internal state, a settled, grounded sense of who you are that holds steady even when the world around you gets loud, critical, or unpredictable. That kind of security isn't something you're born with. It's something you build, deliberately, one small action at a time.

That's exactly what this phase is about.

By the time you reach Phase 7, you've done a significant amount of inner work. You've examined your beliefs, mapped your identity, cleaned your perceptual lens, named your values, and started moving toward what genuinely lights you up. All of that work has been building toward something specific: a version of you that doesn't need the outside world to confirm your worth before you can function well in it. A version of you that can hear criticism without crumbling, set boundaries without guilt, and show up fully in difficult situations without losing yourself in the process.

This is where that version starts to become real.

Foundations of Self-Security

Self-security starts with one honest question: where are you currently getting your sense of worth from?

Most people, if they're being truthful, are getting it from somewhere outside themselves. From their job performance. From how their relationships are going. From whether people around them seem pleased with them. From the number in their bank account or the title on their business card. None of these sources are bad things to care about. The problem is when they become the foundation of your worth rather than simply things in your life. Because all of them can change. All of them can be taken away. And if your sense of self is sitting on top of any of them, it goes down when they do.

Think about a hypothetical scenario: imagine someone like
Thomas, a 36-year-old product director who had built his entire sense of
self around being the sharpest person in the room. He was smart, fast,
and had a track record of being right. His confidence felt solid because it
was constantly being confirmed. Then he moved into a new senior role
surrounded by people who were just as sharp, sometimes sharper.
Suddenly, the confirmation stopped coming as reliably. He started
second-guessing himself in meetings. He got defensive when his ideas
were challenged. He worked longer hours trying to stay ahead. What he
thought was confidence turned out to be a performance that needed an
audience. Without the applause, the whole thing felt shaky. Thomas
didn't have a competence problem. He had a self-security problem. His
worth was rented, not owned.

Owning your worth means separating it from what you produce,
what you achieve, and what other people think of you. It means
connecting to the parts of yourself that exist regardless of your last result.
Your character. Your values. Your way of treating people. Your capacity
to learn and grow. These things don't fluctuate with your quarterly
performance. They're yours regardless of what's happening around you.

The first practice for building this foundation is what's called the
Self-Respect Inventory. This isn't about listing your accomplishments.
It's about identifying the qualities and behaviors you genuinely respect in
yourself. Not what you're proud of in the way you'd tell someone at a
dinner party. What you actually respect about who you are when no one's
watching.

Here's how to do it. Open your journal and write the heading:
"Three things I genuinely respect about myself today." Then write three
specific things. Not vague statements like "I'm a good person." Specific
ones. "I told the truth in a conversation today even though it was
uncomfortable." "I followed through on a commitment I made to myself
this week." "I stayed calm in a situation that would have rattled me six
months ago." The specificity is what gives this exercise its power. You're
not building a fantasy. You're building a record of real evidence that you
are someone worth respecting. Do this every single day. Not as a

motivational exercise. As an evidence-gathering practice. Over weeks, that record becomes something you can actually stand on.

Affirming your identity is the next layer. Your identity is your core sense of who you are, and when you anchor yourself in it regularly, you become less vulnerable to the push and pull of other people's opinions. This doesn't mean you stop caring what others think. It means their assessment stops being the primary source of information you use to evaluate yourself.

A specific way to do this is through what you might call a grounding statement. This is a two or three sentence description of who you are at your core, written in first-person present tense, that you read to yourself at the start of each day. It's not a wish list. It's a statement of what's already true about you. Something like: "I am someone who shows up honestly, works hard, and genuinely cares about the people around me. I make mistakes and I learn from them. My worth isn't up for negotiation." Write yours today. Make it specific to you. Make it something you can actually believe, even on a hard day. Then read it out loud every morning for the next seven days and notice what shifts.

Criticism is one of the biggest tests of self-security, and it's worth spending real time here because most people handle it in one of two unhelpful ways. They either collapse under it, treating every piece of negative feedback as confirmation of their worst fears about themselves, or they deflect it entirely, getting defensive and dismissing anything that challenges their self-image. Both responses have the same root: the belief that criticism says something fundamental about your worth as a person. It doesn't.

Criticism is information. That's the reframe that changes everything about how you receive it. When a colleague tells you that your presentation missed the mark, they're giving you data about the presentation. They're not issuing a verdict on your character. When a client says your proposal wasn't quite what they were looking for, that's information about the proposal. Separating the feedback from your identity isn't about being emotionally detached. It's about being precise.

You can take the useful parts of critical feedback, the parts that actually help you improve, without letting it touch the core of who you are.

Here's a concrete process for handling criticism in the moment. When feedback lands and you feel the instinct to either shut down or push back, do three things before you respond. First, take one slow breath and create a two-second pause between the feedback and your reaction. Second, ask yourself one internal question: "Is there anything useful here that I can actually learn from?" Third, respond with acknowledgment before evaluation. "Thank you for that. Let me think about it." That's it. You don't have to agree. You don't have to defend yourself. You just receive it without letting it define you, and then you decide later, from a calmer place, what to do with it.

Confidence built this way, through daily self-respect, through a grounded identity, through the ability to handle feedback without collapsing, is genuinely different from the kind that depends on external confirmation. It's slower to build. But it doesn't disappear when the applause stops. It's yours regardless of what anyone else says or does.

Small wins are the building blocks of this kind of confidence. Not the big victories that everyone notices. The small ones that only you know about. Finishing the task you kept putting off. Speaking up when you would have stayed quiet. Saying no to something that drains you. Keeping a commitment you made to yourself. Each of these is a vote for the person you're becoming. Each one adds a piece of evidence to the case that you are someone who follows through, who respects themselves, who can be trusted by themselves. That evidence compounds. Over the course of this takeover, it becomes a foundation that can hold real weight.

Don't wait for a grand achievement to feel confident. Track the small ones. Write them down. Give them the weight they deserve. Because confidence isn't built in the moments when everything goes right. It's built in the moments when you show up anyway, even when it's hard, even when you're uncertain, and you do the thing in front of you.

The real test of self-security isn't how you feel when you're alone. It's how you feel when you're around other people, especially the ones who challenge you, pressure you, or have a habit of making you feel like you need to earn your place in the room.

Self-worth, as a concept, gets talked about a lot. But what it actually means in practice is this: your value as a person isn't determined by your performance, your productivity, your relationship status, your income, or anyone's opinion of you. It's inherent. It exists because you exist. That's not a feel-good slogan. It's a foundational belief that, when you actually hold it, changes how you move through every interaction you have.

Consider a hypothetical scenario: imagine someone like Camille, a 32-year-old entrepreneur who had just watched her first business fail after two years of serious effort. The failure was public enough that people in her professional network knew about it. She'd put her whole identity into that business, and when it went under, she felt like she'd gone under with it. She stopped reaching out to people. She turned down invitations. She told herself she had nothing to offer until she'd rebuilt something worth talking about. What she was experiencing wasn't just disappointment. It was what happens when your sense of worth is tied entirely to your results. The moment the results disappeared, so did her sense of having any value. It took her several months of deliberate inner work to separate the failure of the business from any verdict on her as a person. Her intelligence hadn't failed. Her resilience hadn't failed. Her capacity to learn, to care, to try again from a more informed place, none of that had failed. The business failed. She hadn't. That distinction, once she really felt it rather than just understood it intellectually, changed everything about how she rebuilt.

Maintaining self-worth in relationships means carrying that distinction into every interaction. You don't need someone to validate your idea before you trust it. You don't need someone to approve of your decision before you make it. You don't need someone to confirm that you belong in a room before you act like you do. This doesn't mean ignoring feedback or closing yourself off from other people's perspectives. It means that the final authority on your worth isn't out there. It's in here.

There's a specific kind of relationship dynamic that challenges self-worth more than most: the person who consistently makes you feel small. This might be a manager who dismisses your contributions. A family member who questions every choice you make. A colleague who subtly undermines your confidence. A partner who uses criticism as a form of control. These people exist in almost every professional and personal life, and how you respond to them says a lot about where your self-worth is actually anchored.

The key is understanding that other people's behavior toward you is information about them, not about you. Someone who consistently dismisses your ideas is telling you something about their own insecurities or communication style. Someone who makes you feel like you have to earn your place is telling you something about how they were taught to see relationships. You don't have to take their behavior personally, and you don't have to internalize it as truth. You do, however, have to decide what you're willing to accept and what you're not.

That decision is where boundaries come in.

A boundary isn't a wall. It's not an ultimatum. It's not aggression. A boundary is a clear, calm statement of what you will and won't accept, rooted in your values and your self-respect. When you set a boundary from that place, it doesn't feel like an attack. It feels like integrity. And the people in your life who are worth keeping will respect it, even if they push back at first.

Here's a practical process for setting a boundary in a real situation. First, identify specifically what's happening that's draining your energy or violating your sense of self-respect. Be precise. Not "this relationship is exhausting." Name the exact behavior or pattern. Second, decide what you need instead. What would this situation look like if it were working for you? Third, communicate the boundary clearly and calmly, without over-explaining or apologizing for it. "I'm not available for calls after 7 p.m." "I need feedback delivered directly to me, not through other people." "I'm not going to continue this conversation when it becomes personal." You're not asking for permission. You're stating a need. Fourth, follow through. A boundary that isn't enforced isn't a boundary. It's a suggestion. The first time you hold it, especially when someone tests it, is the most important moment. That's when the boundary becomes real.

Saying no is one of the most direct expressions of self-worth there is. Every time you say yes to something that drains you, you're telling yourself, at some level, that your energy isn't worth protecting. Every time you say no from a grounded, values-based place, you're doing the opposite. You're saying that what you have to give matters, and you're choosing where to give it deliberately.

This doesn't mean saying no to everything or becoming unavailable to the people who matter to you. It means being honest about your capacity and your priorities. It means recognizing that saying yes to everything isn't generosity. It's often a fear of conflict or a need for approval dressed up as helpfulness. Real generosity comes from a full cup. And you can't keep a full cup if you never protect what's in it.

Authentic connection, the kind that actually nourishes you rather than depleting you, is only possible when you're secure enough in yourself to show up honestly. When you're performing, managing how you're perceived, suppressing what you actually think to avoid conflict, you can be in a room full of people and still feel completely alone. Security in yourself is what makes real connection possible, because it means you can be seen as you actually are, not as the version you think people want.

Empathy and listening are also part of maintaining self-worth in relationships, in a way that might not be immediately obvious. When you're insecure, you listen defensively. You're scanning for threats, for signs that someone doesn't respect you, for evidence that confirms your fears. When you're secure, you can listen openly. You can hear something that challenges you without feeling attacked. You can hold space for someone else's experience without losing your own. That kind of listening builds the deepest kind of trust, and it's only available to you when you're not too busy protecting yourself to be present for someone else.

Your self-worth isn't up for negotiation. Not in a meeting room, not in a difficult conversation, not in a relationship that's testing you. It's a given. The work of this section is to make that truth so solid inside you that no external circumstance can shake it loose. That's not arrogance. That's the foundation everything else in your life gets built on.

Your Next Move

Phase 7 has been about one thing at its core: moving the source of your worth from the outside to the inside. Everything else in this takeover, the habits you're building, the leadership you're developing, the purpose you're clarifying, all of it becomes more stable when it's resting on a foundation of genuine self-security. You can't lead others from a place of need. You can't build something lasting when your confidence collapses every time someone disagrees with you. You can't show up fully in relationships when you're constantly managing how you're perceived. Self-security isn't a soft skill. It's the infrastructure everything else runs on.

The key takeaways from this phase are worth naming clearly. Your worth isn't tied to your performance or anyone's opinion of you. It's inherent and it's constant. Criticism is information, not a verdict on your character. Confidence is built through small, consistent actions, not through waiting for grand achievements. Healthy boundaries are how you protect your energy and your self-respect in relationships. And affirming your identity daily, through a grounding statement and a self-respect inventory, is how you keep the foundation solid even when life gets hard.

These aren't concepts to agree with and move on from. They're practices to build into your daily life starting right now.

Here are three specific actions to complete before you move into Phase 8.

The first action is to create and use your self-affirming mantra. Write a grounding statement that's two to three sentences long, specific to you, and grounded in what's already true about your character. Write it in present tense. Make it something you can actually believe, even on a difficult day. Then say it out loud every morning for the next seven days, before you check your phone, before you open your laptop, before the day starts pulling your attention outward. This takes less than sixty seconds. Do it standing in front of a mirror if you can. The combination of hearing your own voice say it and seeing yourself say it activates something different than just reading it silently. By day seven, notice whether it starts to feel less like something you're reciting and more like something you simply know.

The second action is to say no to one request this week that drains your energy. Not a huge, dramatic no. Just one clear, calm no to one thing that you would normally agree to out of habit, obligation, or the desire to avoid conflict. Before you say it, identify the specific value or need you're protecting. Then say it without a lengthy explanation or an apology. "I'm not able to take that on right now." "That doesn't work for me." After you say it, write down how it felt. Most people feel a mix of relief and guilt the first time they do this. That's normal. The guilt tends to fade. The relief tends to grow. That shift is your nervous system learning that protecting your energy is safe.

The third action is to write down three things you genuinely respect about yourself today. Not accomplishments. Qualities, behaviors, or choices that reflect who you actually are. Be specific. Then read them out loud. Do this again tomorrow. And the day after. Make it a daily practice for the remainder of this takeover. You're building a record of evidence that you are someone worth respecting. That record, accumulated over days and weeks, becomes the most reliable foundation for self-security that exists. Not what someone else said about you. Not what you achieved last quarter. What you actually know to be true about yourself, from your own direct observation, day after day.

Self-security isn't a destination you arrive at once and stay in forever. It's a practice. It gets stronger with consistent attention and weaker with neglect. The three actions above are how you keep it strong. Do them. Not perfectly. Just consistently.

Phase 8: Stepping Into Authentic Leadership

You've spent seven phases doing something most people never do. You've looked at yourself honestly. You've examined what drives you, what limits you, what you value, and what you're genuinely passionate about. You've built a foundation of self-security that doesn't depend on what other people think of you. All of that work was necessary. And now it points directly toward something bigger than yourself.

Leadership.

Not the kind that comes with a title on a business card. Not the kind that's about being in charge or having authority over other people. The kind that comes from knowing who you are, showing up consistently, and making the people around you better simply by how you operate. That's authentic leadership, and it's available to anyone willing to do the work you've already been doing.

The shift from personal development to leadership isn't as large as it might seem. Every skill you've built in the previous seven phases, your self-awareness, your ability to handle criticism, your clarity about your values, your capacity to listen deeply, all of it feeds directly into how you lead. You were already preparing for this. You just didn't have the label for it yet.

Phase 8 is where that preparation becomes visible to the world around you.

Leading Yourself First

Before you can lead anyone else, you have to lead yourself. This isn't a motivational phrase. It's a practical reality that most people skip over because it's less exciting than the idea of inspiring a team or casting a big vision. But every leader who has ever lost the trust of their people, every manager who has ever been called inconsistent or hypocritical, every entrepreneur who has ever watched a team fall apart, almost always traces the problem back to the same root. They hadn't mastered themselves first.

Self-leadership means governing your own thoughts, emotions, actions, and habits with the same intention and discipline you'd bring to leading others. It means showing up as your best self not just when people are watching, but especially when they're not. It means your behavior on a Tuesday morning when you're tired and behind on emails looks the same as your behavior when you're presenting to a room full of people you want to impress. That consistency is the thing people actually follow. Not your title. Not your vision statement. You.

Think about a hypothetical scenario: imagine someone like Devon, a 38-year-old operations manager at a growing logistics company. Devon was well-liked and smart. His team respected his technical knowledge. But he had a pattern that was quietly eroding his credibility. He'd set expectations in team meetings, clear and specific ones, and then not follow through on his own commitments. He'd tell his team that communication was a priority and then go two days without responding to messages. He'd talk about work-life balance and then send emails at 11 p.m. with an unspoken expectation of a quick reply. He wasn't a bad person. He just hadn't turned his attention to leading himself with the same care he put into managing his team. The gap between what he said and what he did was small, but his team felt it every day. Trust doesn't erode all at once. It erodes in small, repeated moments where words and actions don't match.

The starting point for self-leadership is your daily takeover, the routines and habits you've been building throughout this program. Look at what you've committed to. Are you following it? Not perfectly, but consistently. Because your team, your colleagues, and the people around you are always watching how you treat your own commitments. If you don't take your own structure seriously, you're signaling to everyone around you that structure isn't really that important. And that signal travels faster than any memo you'll ever send.

There's a specific exercise for this called the Self-Governance Audit. It takes about fifteen minutes and you should do it right now, before you move past this section. Open your journal and draw three columns. Label the first column "What I've committed to." Label the second column "What I'm actually doing." Label the third column "The gap." In the first column, write down the key habits, routines, and behavioral standards you've set for yourself over the course of this takeover. Things like your morning routine, your awareness check-ins, your self-talk practice, your boundary-setting. In the second column, write honestly what you're actually doing. Not what you intend to do. What you're doing. In the third column, write the gap between the two. Don't judge it. Just see it clearly.

The gaps you find aren't failures. They're your development edges. They're the specific places where your self-leadership needs more attention. Pick the single largest gap on your list and make it your focus for the next seven days. Not all the gaps. One. Closing one gap fully is worth far more than making vague progress on five of them.

Managing your emotional state is another core component of leading yourself. When you're reactive, when you let frustration drive your decisions or let anxiety make you avoid difficult conversations, you're not leading. You're being led, by your emotions, and that's a problem for everyone around you. The people you work with and live with need to be able to predict how you'll show up. Consistency in your emotional state, not flatness, but groundedness, is one of the most powerful things a leader can offer. It creates safety. It tells people that they can bring you real problems without worrying about how you'll react.

The Centering Breath Takeover you've been using since the introduction becomes especially important here. Use it before difficult conversations. Use it before important decisions. Use it when you feel your emotional state shifting in a direction that won't serve you or the people around you. It's not a trick. It's a tool. And leaders who use it consistently make better decisions, have better conversations, and create better environments than those who don't.

Self-leadership also means being honest about your weaknesses without being paralyzed by them. You already know from Phase 1 that limiting beliefs can masquerade as realistic self-assessment. The same thing applies here. Saying "I'm not a natural communicator" and using it as a reason to avoid difficult conversations is not self-awareness. It's self-protection. Real self-awareness means seeing your weaknesses clearly and then deciding what you're going to do about them. You don't have to be perfect at everything. You do have to be honest about where you need to grow and intentional about doing the growing.

Pick one weakness you know is affecting how you show up for the people around you. Not your biggest, most overwhelming one. One specific, manageable one. Write it down. Then write one concrete action you can take this week to start addressing it. Not a plan to fix it entirely. One step. That step is your self-leadership in action.

The discipline of showing up as your best self, day after day, even when it's inconvenient, even when no one would notice if you didn't, is what builds the credibility that makes people want to follow you. You can't manufacture that credibility. You can only earn it, one consistent action at a time. And you've been doing exactly that for the past seven phases. Phase 8 is where you start to see that it was never just about you.

Vision, Influence, and Trust

A leader without a vision is just a person with authority. Authority can make people comply. Vision makes people commit. Those are completely different things, and the difference shows up every time the work gets hard.

Vision is the clearest picture you can paint of where you're going and why it matters. It's not a mission statement. It's not a list of goals. It's a compelling description of a future that people can see themselves in, one that's specific enough to be real and meaningful enough to be worth working toward. When your vision is clear and you can communicate it well, people don't just understand what you're doing. They feel why it matters. And when people feel why something matters, they bring a completely different quality of energy to it.

The North Star principle is useful here. A North Star doesn't tell you every step of the path. It gives you a fixed point to orient toward when you're uncertain about which direction to move. Your vision works the same way. It doesn't need to answer every question. It needs to be clear enough that when a decision comes up, you and the people around you can ask: does this move us toward the vision or away from it? That question alone simplifies a huge number of decisions that would otherwise feel complicated.

Here's how to build and articulate a clear vision for something specific in your life right now. It doesn't have to be a company or a massive project. It can be a team you lead, a department you're part of, a side project, or even your family. Pick one context where you have some degree of influence. Then answer these three questions in writing. First: what does success look like in this context twelve months from now? Be specific. Name the actual outcomes, behaviors, and conditions you want to see. Second: why does that future matter, to you and to the people involved? What does it make possible that isn't possible right now? Third: what's the one thing that would have to be true for that future to happen? That third answer usually points directly at the most important thing to focus on.

Once you have those three answers, write a single paragraph that captures the vision. Read it out loud. Does it feel real? Does it feel worth working toward? If it feels flat or generic, it needs more specificity. A vision that doesn't move you won't move anyone else either.

Influence is the natural result of a clear vision communicated well. But it's worth being precise about what influence actually means, because it gets confused with manipulation more often than it should. Manipulation works by exploiting people's fears, insecurities, or lack of information to get them to do what you want. Influence works by helping people see a future they genuinely want to be part of and showing them how their contribution matters to getting there. One of these approaches extracts energy from people. The other generates it. The difference in long-term outcomes is enormous.

Real influence has three components. The first is clarity. You can't inspire people with a fuzzy idea. The more clearly you can describe what you're working toward, the more easily people can decide whether they're in. The second is connection. People need to see how the vision connects to something they personally care about. This isn't manipulation. It's good communication. If someone on your team cares deeply about growth and learning, showing them how the vision creates opportunities for that is honest and relevant. If someone values stability, showing them how the vision builds something sustainable speaks to what matters to them. You're not changing the vision. You're translating it. The third component is consistency. You can't cast a vision once and expect it to hold. You have to keep coming back to it. Keep referencing it in decisions. Keep showing how the daily work connects to the bigger picture. Influence isn't a speech. It's a sustained practice.

Think about a hypothetical scenario: imagine someone like Yara, a 35-year-old team lead at a marketing agency. Her team was technically capable but had been running on low morale for months. The work felt disconnected, like a series of tasks rather than something that added up to anything meaningful. Yara had never thought of herself as a "visionary" type. She was practical, detail-oriented, and a little skeptical of big-picture talk. But she tried something simple. She called a team meeting and, instead of going through the project list, she talked for ten minutes about what the work they were doing actually made possible for the clients they served. She connected the day-to-day tasks to real outcomes for real people. Then she asked her team what they wanted their work to mean. The conversation that followed was the most engaged that team had been in months. She hadn't changed the work. She'd changed the story around it. That's influence. And it cost her exactly ten minutes of honesty.

Trust is the currency that makes everything else in leadership possible. You can have a clear vision. You can communicate it compellingly. But if people don't trust you, none of it lands. They'll nod along and do the minimum. They won't bring you their real problems. They won't take risks or share honest ideas. They'll manage up instead of working with you. A team without trust is a group of individuals protecting themselves. A team with trust is something completely different.

Trust is built through one thing more than any other: consistency between what you say and what you do. Every time you say you'll do something and then do it, you make a deposit. Every time you say one thing and do another, you make a withdrawal. The account balance of trust in any relationship, professional or personal, is just the running total of those deposits and withdrawals over time. There's no shortcut. There's no speech that builds trust the way consistent behavior does.

Transparency is a major component of this. People don't need you to have all the answers. They need to know you're being straight with them. When you share relevant information honestly, even when it's uncomfortable, you signal that you respect the people around you enough to treat them as adults. When you withhold information or soften things beyond recognition, people sense it. They fill the gap with assumptions that are almost always worse than the truth. Being transparent doesn't mean sharing everything indiscriminately. It means sharing what's relevant, honestly, without spin.

Here's a specific practice for building trust this week. Identify one piece of relevant information that you've been holding back from your team, a colleague, or someone in your personal life. Not something that would cause harm to share. Something that you've been keeping close because it feels uncomfortable or uncertain. Share it. Be straightforward about what you know and what you don't. Notice how the other person responds. In most cases, honesty, even about uncertain things, creates more trust than polished reassurance ever does.

Servant leadership is the model that ties vision, influence, and trust together into something coherent and sustainable. The core idea is simple: your job as a leader isn't to be served by the people around you. It's to serve them. To remove the obstacles in their way. To help them develop. To create the conditions where they can do their best work. This doesn't mean you have no standards or that you absorb everyone else's problems. It means your primary question shifts from "what do I need?" to "what does this person need to succeed?"

That shift changes everything about how you show up. When you walk into a meeting as a servant leader, you're not there to demonstrate your competence. You're there to help the people in the room move forward. When someone on your team is struggling, your first instinct isn't to judge the performance. It's to ask what's getting in the way. When someone does something well, you say so specifically and publicly.

When something goes wrong, you take your share of the responsibility rather than looking for someone to blame.

Humility is the quality that makes servant leadership real rather than performative. And humility doesn't mean thinking less of yourself. It means thinking about yourself less. It means being genuinely curious about other people's perspectives, genuinely willing to be wrong, and genuinely invested in the success of the people around you rather than just your own. That kind of humility is actually a strength. It makes you more accurate, because you're not filtering information through ego. It makes you more trusted, because people know you're not just listening for confirmation. And it makes you more effective, because you're working with reality rather than the version of reality your ego prefers.

The B.O.S.S. principles you've been building throughout this takeover, the self-awareness, the values clarity, the emotional regulation, the identity work, all of it converges here. Authentic leadership isn't a separate skill set you add on top of everything else. It's the natural expression of everything you've been developing. When you know yourself, govern yourself, communicate your vision clearly, build trust through consistency, and put the growth of the people around you at the center of how you operate, you're not just a better leader. You're a fundamentally different kind of person to be around. And that difference creates ripple effects that go far beyond any single team, project, or organization.

Leadership at this level isn't loud. It doesn't need to be. It shows up in the quality of your attention, the reliability of your follow-through, the honesty of your communication, and the genuine care you bring to the people in your sphere. Those things are felt before they're seen. And they're remembered long after any title or achievement has faded.

Putting It Into Practice

Phase 8 has covered the full arc of authentic leadership, from the inside out. Self-governance first. Vision and influence second. Trust and service third. These aren't separate topics. They're a sequence. Each one builds on the one before it. You can't build real trust without the consistency that comes from leading yourself. You can't influence effectively without the trust that makes people actually listen. And you can't sustain any of it without the servant mindset that keeps the whole thing grounded in something bigger than your own advancement.

The work now is to take what you've read and put it into motion today, with specific actions that produce real outcomes rather than just good intentions.

The first action is to complete the Self-Governance Audit described in the first section. Do it fully. Three columns. Honest answers. Identify your single largest gap between what you've committed to and what you're actually doing. Write one concrete action you'll take every day for the next seven days to close that specific gap. Put it in your calendar. Not as a reminder. As an appointment with yourself that you treat with the same respect you'd give a meeting with someone you want to impress.

The second action is to write your vision paragraph for one specific context in your life where you have influence. Use the three questions from this chapter: what does success look like twelve months from now, why does that future matter, and what one thing has to be true for it to happen. Write the paragraph. Read it out loud. Then share it with one person who's part of that context. Not to get their approval. To practice articulating it clearly and to invite them into it. Ask them one question after you share it: "Is there anything about this that doesn't connect with what you care about?" Their answer will tell you where your vision needs to be clearer or more inclusive.

The third action is to identify one way you can serve a team member, colleague, or person in your life today, without being asked. Not a grand gesture. Something specific and useful. Help them with something they're stuck on. Remove an obstacle that's slowing them down. Acknowledge something they've done well, in specific terms, directly to them. Then do it. Today. The act of serving someone without being asked, especially when you're busy or have your own pressures, is one of the most direct expressions of servant leadership there is. It's also one of the fastest ways to build the kind of trust that doesn't need to be asked for. It just shows up.

The fourth action is to evaluate your consistency in one daily routine you've committed to during this takeover. Not all of them. One. Ask yourself honestly: am I doing this because I believe in it, or am I doing it when it's convenient? If the answer is "when it's convenient," that's your work. Consistency isn't about perfection. It's about showing up for the things you've said matter to you, especially on the days when it would be easy not to. That's where character gets built. That's where the credibility that makes authentic leadership possible comes from.

The 98-Day Superior Self Takeover was always building toward this. Not just a better version of you in isolation, but a version of you that makes the people around you better too. That's the full picture of what total life redesign actually means. It's not just your habits, your mindset, or your daily routine. It's the quality of your presence in every room you walk into, every conversation you have, and every commitment you make and keep. That presence, built through 98 days of deliberate, consistent action, is what authentic leadership actually looks like in real life.

Phase 9: Mastering Habits for Success

Habits are the invisible architecture of your life. Every morning routine, every automatic reaction, every pattern you run without thinking, these are the building blocks of who you are right now. And here's what's true about building blocks: you can rearrange them. You can swap out the ones that aren't working and replace them with ones that actually serve the life you're building. That's exactly what this phase is about.

You're now at day 57 of the 98-Day Superior Self Takeover. You've done the identity work, the values work, the self-awareness work. You've examined what drives you and what holds you back. All of that was necessary, because you can't build strong habits on top of a foundation you haven't examined. But now it's time to take everything you've learned about yourself and put it into daily structure. Habits are where insight becomes action. They're where the person you want to be starts showing up in the person you actually are each day.

This phase has four sections. First, you'll learn how to build new habits without blowing up your current life. Second, you'll identify the specific habits that are quietly working against you and learn a concrete system for replacing them. Third, you'll build the accountability structure that keeps you consistent through the hardest stretch of this takeover. And fourth, you'll walk away with clear action steps you can start today.

The Science of Habit Stacking

Most people try to build new habits the hard way. They decide they want to meditate, exercise, journal, and drink more water, all starting Monday. By Wednesday, the plan has collapsed. Not because they're lazy or undisciplined. Because they tried to add too much, too fast, to a brain that treats unfamiliar routines as threats to its efficiency.

Your brain loves patterns. It runs on them. Every habit you have, good or bad, exists because your brain automated it to save energy. That's not a flaw. It's a feature. The key is learning how to use that feature intentionally, so you're building the habits you actually want rather than just running the ones that formed by accident.

This is where Micro-Action Stacking comes in.

Micro-Action Stacking is the practice of attaching a new, small behavior to an existing routine you already do automatically. Instead of trying to carve out a brand new slot in your day, you piggyback the new habit onto something that's already happening. Your brain doesn't have to work as hard to adopt it, because it's already anchored to a familiar cue. The existing habit becomes the trigger. The new habit becomes the response that follows.

Think about how this works in practice. You already make coffee every morning. That's a locked-in routine. Now, while the coffee brews, you spend two minutes writing three things you're grateful for. The coffee-making didn't change. You just attached something new to it. After a few weeks, making coffee and writing in your gratitude journal feel like one continuous sequence. The new habit has been absorbed into the existing one. That's the mechanism. Simple, but genuinely powerful when applied consistently.

The reason small changes beat massive overhauls isn't just psychological. It's biological. When you make a dramatic change all at once, your stress response activates. Your nervous system reads the disruption as a threat. Resistance goes up. Willpower gets depleted fast. But when you make a tiny change attached to something familiar, the disruption is minimal. The brain adapts without fighting you. Over time, those tiny changes compound into something significant. That's not a motivational idea. That's how neural pathways actually form.

Here's the exact process for building a habit stack. Start by listing five to seven things you already do every single day without thinking. Wake up, brush your teeth, make coffee, sit down at your desk, eat lunch, check your phone before bed. These are your anchor habits. They're the hooks you'll attach new behaviors to. Write them down in the order they happen.

Next, pick one new habit you want to build. Just one. Not three. One. Make it small enough that it takes two minutes or less to complete. You can always expand it later, but starting small is what gets it to stick. Now choose the anchor habit that makes the most logical sense as a trigger. If you want to build a reading habit, attach it to your lunch break. If you want to build a daily planning habit, attach it to sitting down at your desk in the morning. If you want to add a short breathing practice, attach it to your morning coffee. The pairing should feel natural, not forced.

Write the stack as a formula: "After I [anchor habit], I will [new habit]." That sentence structure is important. It creates a specific, predictable cue-response sequence in your brain. "After I sit down at my desk in the morning, I will spend two minutes writing my top three priorities for the day." That's a habit stack. Concrete. Specific. Attached to something that already happens.

Do this for seven consecutive days before you evaluate it. Don't adjust it after day two because it feels awkward. Awkward is normal. The brain is building a new pathway, and new pathways feel uncomfortable before they feel automatic. Give it the full seven days. After a week, ask yourself two questions: did I do it at least five out of seven days? Did the new behavior feel slightly more natural by day seven than it did on day one? If yes to both, you have a working habit stack. Keep it for another three weeks before you add anything new.

The Visual Progress Map is the tool that makes all of this visible. You've been tracking your progress through this takeover on the map since week one. Now, in week nine, your habit stacks get their own row. Each day you complete your stack, you check it off. That check mark isn't just administrative. It's a small but real piece of evidence that the new version of you is showing up. Over days and weeks, those check marks accumulate into something you can see. Visible progress is motivating in a way that invisible progress never is. You're not just feeling like you're changing. You're watching yourself change, one day at a time.

One more thing about habit stacking that's worth being clear on: the goal isn't to build a perfect morning routine that takes two hours. The goal is to build two or three small, consistent behaviors that compound over the 98-day takeover into something genuinely different. Two minutes of daily planning, done every day for 41 remaining days, produces more real change than a three-hour planning session done once. Consistency beats intensity. Always.

Breaking the Loops of Sabotage

Building new habits is one side of this work. The other side is harder, and most people avoid it. It's looking honestly at the habits that are quietly costing you.

Every person reading this has at least one automatic behavior that works against their goals. Maybe it's reaching for your phone the moment you feel bored or anxious, which breaks your focus and keeps you in a state of shallow attention all day. Maybe it's saying yes to everything, which leaves you exhausted and resentful by Thursday. Maybe it's the late-night snacking, the procrastination spiral, the checking of social media as a substitute for doing the thing you're avoiding. These aren't character flaws. They're loops. And loops have a structure you can identify and interrupt.

Every habit, good or bad, follows the same three-part sequence: a trigger, a behavior, and a reward. The trigger is the cue that starts the loop. The behavior is the automatic action. The reward is what the behavior gives you, even if it's something small like momentary relief or a brief distraction from discomfort. Understanding this sequence is how you break the loop, because you can't interrupt something you haven't mapped.

Consider a hypothetical scenario: imagine someone like Aaron, a 33-year-old account manager who kept telling himself he'd stop mindlessly scrolling his phone during the first thirty minutes of his workday. He tried blocking apps. He tried leaving his phone in another room. Nothing stuck for more than a few days. When he actually mapped the loop, he discovered the trigger wasn't boredom. It was the mild anxiety he felt every morning when he sat down and saw his to-do list. The scrolling wasn't laziness. It was a way of delaying the discomfort of facing a heavy workload. The reward was temporary relief from that anxiety. Once Aaron saw the real trigger, he stopped trying to fight the phone and started addressing the anxiety directly. He added a two-minute breathing practice right after sitting down at his desk, before opening anything. Within two weeks, the scrolling dropped significantly. He hadn't white-knuckled his way through willpower. He'd replaced the trigger's usual response with a better one.

That's the system. You don't just remove a bad habit. You replace it. The brain needs the loop to close. If you take away the behavior without offering an alternative, the trigger still fires and the need for a reward still exists. The loop finds another way to close, often through a behavior that's just as unhelpful as the original one. Replacement is the key.

Here's the exact process for breaking a sabotage loop. Step one: identify the habit you want to change. Be specific. Not "I want to stop being unproductive." Name the exact behavior. "I check social media on my phone for twenty minutes every morning before I start real work."

Step two: identify the trigger. Ask yourself: what's happening right before this behavior occurs? What time of day is it? What are you feeling in your body? What situation or emotion precedes it? Write down your answer. The trigger is usually one of five things: a specific time, a location, an emotional state, another person, or an immediately preceding action. Most people's triggers are emotional states they haven't fully named yet.

Step three: identify the reward. Ask yourself: what does this behavior give me, even briefly? Relief from discomfort? A sense of connection? A feeling of control? A temporary escape? Be honest. There's always a reward, even for habits you hate. Naming it tells you what need the habit is actually meeting, and that tells you what the replacement needs to provide.

Step four: design the replacement. Find a behavior that meets the same need in a way that doesn't work against your goals. If the reward is relief from anxiety, a breathing practice or a two-minute walk might serve the same function. If the reward is a sense of connection, a brief check-in with a colleague might work better than scrolling. The replacement doesn't have to be perfect. It just has to address the same underlying need and be something you can actually do in the moment the trigger fires.

Step five: practice the replacement deliberately for fourteen days. Every time the trigger fires, you interrupt the old behavior and run the new one. You won't succeed every time. You don't have to. Aim for seven out of ten. That's enough to start weakening the old pathway and strengthening the new one. After fourteen days, evaluate. Is the old behavior less automatic? Does the replacement feel slightly more natural? If yes, you're on track. Keep going.

Awareness is the foundation of all of this. You can't break a loop you're running unconsciously. The single most important first step is simply noticing the habit happening in real time, not after the fact, not in a reflection session at the end of the day, but in the actual moment it starts. That moment of noticing is where your power lives. Before you notice, the loop just runs. After you notice, you have a choice. Building that noticing muscle is the work of the first week of this process, and it's worth doing before you try to change anything at all.

For the next three days, before you attempt any replacement, just watch one habit you want to change. Don't try to stop it. Just notice when it starts, what triggered it, and how you feel during and after. Write down what you observe each time. Three days of honest observation will give you more useful information about that habit than any amount of willpower-based resistance ever could.

Accountability and Consistency

You're in the middle weeks of this takeover now. And the middle is where most people quietly fall apart.

The beginning of any 98-day commitment has energy behind it. The novelty, the motivation, the excitement of starting something new, all of it carries you through the first few weeks. The end has its own pull, the finish line, the sense of completion, the proof that you did it. But the middle? The middle has none of that. It's just the work, day after day, without the emotional boost of a beginning or the visible reward of an ending. It's where habits either solidify or quietly dissolve. It's where consistency becomes a choice you have to make deliberately rather than something that happens automatically.

Consistency is the bridge between where you are and where you want to be. That's not a metaphor. It's a functional reality. The habits you're building in this phase only become automatic through repetition. The neural pathways only strengthen through consistent use. The identity shift you're working toward only happens when the new behaviors show up reliably enough that your brain starts treating them as part of who you are. One missed day doesn't break the chain. A week of drift, followed by a month of "I'll get back to it," does.

The middle weeks are where accountability becomes non-negotiable.

Accountability isn't about having someone watch you or report your failures to someone else. It's about having a structure that makes it harder to quietly let things slide without noticing. There are three layers to an effective accountability system, and you need all three working together.

The first layer is self-accountability. This is your daily check-in with your Visual Progress Map. Every evening, before you go to bed, spend three minutes reviewing your day. Ask yourself three specific questions: Did I complete my habit stack today? Did I practice the replacement behavior for my sabotage loop? Did I do one thing today that moves me toward the person I'm becoming? Answer honestly. Check the boxes that deserve to be checked. Leave blank the ones that don't. The map doesn't lie, and that's the point. Over days and weeks, the pattern becomes visible. You'll see whether you're building momentum or slowly drifting. That visibility is accountability in its most honest form.

The second layer is partner accountability. Identify one person in your life who's also working toward something meaningful, a colleague, a friend, a partner, someone in your professional network. It doesn't have to be someone doing this exact takeover. It just has to be someone who takes their own growth seriously. Set up a weekly check-in with this person. Keep it short, ten to fifteen minutes maximum. Each of you shares three things: what you committed to last week, what you actually did, and what you're committing to this week. That's the whole structure. No lengthy discussion required. Just honest reporting and a clear commitment going forward.

The reason this works is simple. When you know you're going to tell someone what you did, you're more likely to do it. Not because you fear judgment, but because saying it out loud to another person makes the commitment real in a way that a private note to yourself doesn't. The act of reporting creates a small but genuine social stake. That stake is often enough to push you through the moments when motivation has dipped and discipline alone isn't quite enough.

The third layer is environmental accountability. This means designing your physical and digital environment to make your habits easier to do and your sabotage loops harder to run. If your habit stack includes a morning journal, put the journal on your pillow the night before so it's the first thing you see when you wake up. If your sabotage loop involves your phone, charge it in a different room overnight. If your new habit requires a specific tool or resource, keep it in the exact spot where the anchor habit happens. Your environment is always nudging you in one direction or another. Make sure it's nudging you in the right one.

There's also the question of what to do when you miss a day. Because you will. That's not pessimism. It's reality. Life interrupts even the best-designed systems. The takeover doesn't ask you to be perfect. It asks you to be consistent over time. The rule here is simple: never miss twice in a row. One missed day is a slip. Two missed days is the beginning of a new pattern. The moment you notice you've missed a day, your only job is to show up the next day. Not to make up for lost ground. Not to beat yourself up. Just to show up the next day and do the thing. That single act of returning is more important than any streak you could maintain.

Think about a hypothetical scenario: imagine someone like Keisha, a 30-year-old marketing director who was three weeks into her habit-building work when a product launch consumed her entire week. She missed her morning routine four days in a row. By Friday, she'd started to tell herself the familiar story: "I've broken the streak, I might as well wait until next week to restart." She caught the thought, recognized it as the same avoidance pattern she'd been working on, and did a five-minute version of her morning routine that Saturday morning. Not the full version. Five minutes. Just enough to close the loop and restart the sequence. The following week, she was back to the full routine. The four missed days didn't define her progress. The decision to return did.

Momentum in the middle weeks isn't about perfect execution. It's about the quality of your returns. How quickly do you come back when you drift? How honest are you with yourself when you check the map? How reliable is your weekly check-in with your accountability partner? These are the behaviors that determine whether the middle weeks build you up or wear you down.

The 98-day commitment you made at the start of this takeover is a promise to yourself. Not to be perfect. To keep showing up. Phase 9 is where that promise gets tested most directly, and where keeping it matters most. Every day you show up in the middle, when there's no novelty and no finish line in sight, you're building something that goes beyond any single habit. You're building the identity of someone who follows through. That identity is the most valuable thing this takeover can give you.

Habits are the architecture of your life. Not your intentions. Not your goals. Your daily behaviors, the ones you run automatically, the ones you've built deliberately, and the ones you've never stopped to examine. These are the structures that determine what your life actually looks like, day after day, year after year. Designing them with care isn't optional if you're serious about total life redesign. It's the work itself.

Phase 9 has given you three specific tools. Micro-Action Stacking lets you build new habits without overwhelming your system. The Sabotage Loop framework lets you identify and replace the behaviors that are quietly working against you. And the three-layer accountability system keeps you consistent through the middle stretch when motivation alone won't carry you.

These tools only work if you use them. Here are your three action steps for this week.

Action Step 1: Choose one new habit and stack it onto a current one. Use the formula from this chapter: "After I [anchor habit], I will [new habit]." Make the new habit take two minutes or less. Write the stack down. Do it for seven consecutive days. Check it off on your Visual Progress Map each day you complete it. Don't add a second stack until the first one feels natural.

Action Step 2: Identify one sabotage habit and map its trigger. Pick one automatic behavior you want to change. Spend three days just observing it, when it happens, what precedes it, and what it gives you. On day four, write the full loop: trigger, behavior, reward. Then design one replacement behavior that meets the same underlying need in a more useful way. Start running the replacement every time the trigger fires. Track your success rate honestly on your map.

Action Step 3: Check off your progress on the Visual Progress Map. Tonight, before you go to bed, open your map. Mark where you are in the takeover. Check off today's habit stack if you completed it. Review the last seven days of entries and ask yourself one honest question: am I building momentum or slowly drifting? If you're drifting, identify the single smallest action you can take tomorrow to return to the path. Then do that action tomorrow, before anything else.

The habits you build in these middle weeks of the takeover aren't just behaviors. They're votes for the person you're becoming. Each check mark on the map is evidence. Each replacement behavior is a decision. Each day you show up is a brick in something real. The architecture of your superior self is being built right now, one small, deliberate action at a time.

Phase 10: The Power of Mindset

You're at day 64. You've built habits, examined your identity, clarified your values, and started leading from a more grounded place. That's real work. And now something shifts. Because everything you've built on the outside, the routines, the structures, the accountability systems, only goes as far as the mindset running underneath it. Your mindset is the operating system. Everything else is software. If the operating system is limited, it doesn't matter how good the software is. It won't run at full capacity.

That's what this phase is about.

Mindset isn't a buzzword. It's the collection of beliefs you hold about yourself, about what's possible, and about what failure and success actually mean. Those beliefs determine what you attempt, how you respond when things go wrong, and whether you keep going or quietly give up. Two people can face the exact same challenge and have completely different outcomes based entirely on the mindset they bring to it. Same situation. Completely different results. That gap is what this chapter closes.

Over the next seven days of this takeover, you'll work through the specific beliefs and practices that shape how your mind operates under pressure. You'll learn to see failure differently, use your imagination as a performance tool, and build a daily gratitude practice that actually changes how your brain processes the world around you. These aren't abstract concepts. Each one has a clear, practical application you can start using today.

Growth vs. Fixed Mindset

There are two fundamentally different ways to see your own abilities. The first is a fixed mindset. This is the belief that your intelligence, talent, and capabilities are set. You either have it or you don't. When things go wrong with a fixed mindset, the conclusion is usually the same: "I'm just not good at this." Failure becomes a verdict. Challenges become threats. Feedback feels like an attack. The fixed mindset avoids difficulty because difficulty exposes limits, and limits feel permanent.

The second way is a growth mindset. This is the belief that your abilities can be developed through effort, learning, and persistence. With a growth mindset, failure isn't a verdict. It's information. A challenge isn't a threat. It's a chance to get better. Feedback isn't an attack. It's data you can use. The growth mindset doesn't mean believing you can do anything with no effort. It means believing that effort actually changes what you're capable of.

Most people operate somewhere between the two, depending on the situation. You might have a growth mindset about your professional skills but a fixed mindset about your social abilities. You might believe you can improve your fitness but secretly believe your creativity is just "not there." The work of this section is to find where your fixed mindset is quietly running the show and start replacing it with something more accurate and more useful.

Think about a hypothetical scenario: imagine someone like Jordan, a 31-year-old project coordinator who had been passed over for a promotion twice. After the second time, Jordan told himself the story that the company just didn't see his value, that leadership roles weren't really for him, that maybe he'd peaked. He stopped volunteering for high-visibility projects. He stopped asking for feedback. He stopped pushing. What looked like acceptance was actually a fixed mindset protecting itself from further disappointment. When Jordan was asked directly what he'd learned from each performance review, he realized he'd never actually processed the feedback. He'd received it, felt the sting, and filed it away without extracting anything useful. The moment he started treating those reviews as data rather than verdicts, everything about how he approached his work shifted. He wasn't suddenly more talented. He was suddenly more teachable. And teachable people grow faster than talented people who've stopped learning.

Beliefs are the blueprints of your life. They dictate what you think is possible and what you're willing to try. A limiting belief doesn't announce itself. It shows up as a reason, a justification, a perfectly logical explanation for why something isn't worth attempting. "I'm not a natural leader." "I've never been good at numbers." "I don't have the right background for that." These thoughts feel like honest self-assessment. They're not. They're conclusions drawn from limited evidence and then repeated until they feel like facts.

The process for challenging a limiting belief is the same one you used in Phase 1, but now you're applying it specifically to your mindset about growth and capability. First, name the belief clearly. Write it down in one sentence. Second, ask what evidence actually supports it. Not feelings. Evidence. Third, ask what evidence contradicts it. Look for the times the belief wasn't true, the moments you surprised yourself, the skills you developed that you once thought were beyond you. Fourth, write a replacement belief that's honest and at least partially believable. Not a fantasy. A more accurate statement that leaves room for growth.

Self-doubt is the voice that shows up right at the edge of your comfort zone. Every time you're about to try something that actually matters to you, it gets louder. "You're not ready." "Who do you think you are?" "You're going to embarrass yourself." That voice isn't a fact-checker. It's a pattern, one that formed to protect you from the discomfort of trying and failing. The problem is that it also protects you from the discomfort of trying and succeeding. It protects you from everything.

Self-doubt is a feeling, not a fact. That distinction matters enormously. A feeling can be acknowledged without being obeyed. When self-doubt shows up, you don't have to argue with it or pretend it isn't there. You acknowledge it and act anyway. The action is the point. Courage isn't the absence of self-doubt. It's what you do while it's present.

Here's the specific practice for this section. Pick one challenge you're currently facing, at work, in a relationship, in a goal you've been putting off. Write down the fixed mindset thought you've been carrying about it. Something like "I'm not cut out for this" or "I don't have what it takes." Then write three specific things you've already learned or improved in this area, even small ones. Then write the growth mindset version of the original thought. "I'm still developing this skill and I have real evidence that I'm capable of growth." Say the new version out loud. Then identify one small action you can take today that proves the growth mindset right, even slightly. Do that action before the day ends.

Failure is feedback. Not comfortable feedback. Not always easy to receive. But feedback. Every setback contains specific information about what didn't work and why. The person who treats failure as a verdict stops collecting that information. The person who treats it as data keeps learning, keeps adjusting, keeps moving. Over the course of a 98-day takeover, the difference between those two approaches is enormous. One person is still on day one in their head, no matter what day the calendar says. The other is genuinely different on day 64 than they were on day one. That difference isn't talent. It's mindset.

Growth is always possible. That's not optimism. That's what the science of neuroplasticity actually shows: your brain continues to form new connections throughout your life in response to learning and experience. You are not a finished product. You are a work in progress, and the direction of that progress is something you have genuine influence over. Starting right now, today, with the belief you choose to carry into the next challenge you face.

Your brain doesn't draw a sharp line between what you vividly imagine and what you actually experience. This isn't a philosophical idea. It's a functional reality about how your nervous system works. When you visualize something with enough detail and emotional intensity, your brain activates many of the same regions it would activate if the event were actually happening. Athletes have used this for decades. Surgeons use it. Performers use it. And you can use it too, starting with a two-minute daily practice that costs nothing and requires no equipment.

Visualization works because mental rehearsal builds the same neural pathways that physical rehearsal builds. When you repeatedly picture yourself handling a difficult conversation with clarity and calm, you're not just daydreaming. You're practicing. When the actual conversation happens, your brain has a reference point. It's been there before, in a sense. The situation feels slightly more familiar, slightly less threatening. That slight shift in familiarity reduces anxiety and increases the quality of your performance.

Think about a hypothetical scenario: imagine someone like Marcus, a 36-year-old operations director who had a major presentation to the company's executive team coming up. He'd given presentations before, but not at this level, and the anxiety was real. For two weeks before the presentation, he spent two minutes each morning visualizing it. Not vaguely. Specifically. He pictured the room, the faces of the people in it, the sound of his own voice coming out steady and clear. He felt the confidence in his posture. He saw the executives nodding as his key points landed. He pictured the questions at the end and himself answering them without flinching. When the actual day came, something was different. The room felt familiar in a way it had no right to feel. The anxiety was still there, but it was manageable. He'd been in that room before, in every way that mattered to his nervous system. He delivered the best presentation of his career. Not because the visualization was magic. Because he'd practiced.

The visualization practice for this section is specific and takes exactly two minutes. Do it every morning for the remainder of this phase.

Here's how. Sit somewhere quiet. Close your eyes. Take three slow breaths to settle your nervous system. Then bring to mind one goal you're actively working toward. See it as already achieved. Not "I hope this happens." See it as done. Picture where you are when it's complete. What does the room look like? Who's there? What are you feeling in your body? What does success sound like in this moment? What does it feel like to have done the thing you set out to do? Hold that image for ninety seconds with as much sensory detail as you can generate. Then open your eyes and take one action toward that goal before you do anything else.

The action piece is critical. Visualization without action is just daydreaming. The purpose of the mental rehearsal is to prime your nervous system and clarify your direction, not to replace the work. The two minutes of visualization point you toward the action. The action is where the result actually gets built.

Affirmations work through a related mechanism. When you say something out loud, repeatedly, in a present-tense, first-person statement, you're feeding your brain a signal about who you are. The brain is always listening for that signal. It uses it to filter information, to direct attention, and to shape behavior. Most people are running affirmations all day long without realizing it. They're just negative ones. "I'm terrible at this." "I always mess this up." "I'm not the kind of person who can do that." These statements function as instructions. The brain follows them.

Positive affirmations aren't about pretending everything is perfect. They're about choosing a more accurate and more useful instruction to give your brain. The key is that they have to feel at least partially believable, or your brain will reject them immediately. "I am the most successful person alive" won't work if you don't believe it even slightly. But "I am someone who learns quickly and gets better with consistent effort" is something most people can actually hold onto. That's the target. Not a fantasy. A grounded, honest statement about who you're becoming.

Write one affirmation that connects directly to your current biggest goal. Make it present tense. Make it first person. Make it specific enough to be meaningful and honest enough to be believable. Something like: "I show up prepared and clear in high-stakes situations." Or: "I make decisions that reflect my values, even when it's uncomfortable." Or: "I am building the discipline and focus that my goals require." Write it down. Say it out loud three times right now. Then say it again tomorrow morning, before you check your phone, before you look at your email, before the day starts pulling your attention outward. Do this every day for the next seven days and notice what shifts in how you approach the goal it's connected to.

The combination of visualization and affirmation is more powerful than either one alone. The visualization gives your brain a vivid, emotionally real picture of where you're going. The affirmation gives it a clear, repeated statement about who you are as you get there. Together, they create an internal environment that supports the external actions you're taking. They don't replace the work. They make the work more likely to happen, and more likely to succeed when it does.

Gratitude as a Performance Tool

Gratitude gets talked about in ways that make it sound soft. Like a nice habit for people who have time to be reflective. That framing misses what gratitude actually does at a functional level. Gratitude isn't just a feeling. It's a cognitive shift. When you deliberately focus on what's working, what you have, and what's going right, your brain starts scanning the environment differently. It starts finding more of those things. That's not wishful thinking. That's how attention and perception actually work.

Your brain has a filtering system called the reticular activating system that determines what you consciously notice out of the overwhelming amount of information available to you at any given moment. It filters based on what you've told it is important. When you're running a mindset of scarcity and anxiety, it finds evidence for that. When you train it to look for what's working, it finds evidence for that instead. Gratitude is one of the most direct ways to reset that filter.

The research on this is consistent. Regular gratitude practice reduces cortisol, the primary stress hormone. It improves sleep quality. It increases resilience after setbacks. It improves focus and decision-making. These aren't small effects. For a working professional or entrepreneur operating under sustained pressure, these are the exact outcomes that determine whether you perform at your best or slowly burn out. Gratitude isn't a luxury. For people operating at high levels, it's a performance tool.

Think about a hypothetical scenario: imagine someone like Priya, a 34-year-old product manager who had a major client presentation in the morning and couldn't sleep. She was cycling through everything that could go wrong. The slides weren't perfect. She wasn't sure the client would respond well to the pricing. She'd been working sixteen-hour days for two weeks and was running on empty. At 11 p.m., instead of continuing to spiral, she opened her notebook and wrote five things she was genuinely grateful for in that moment. Her team had pulled together and delivered solid work. She'd done this kind of presentation before and handled it. She had the full context of the client's needs. She'd eaten a decent dinner. The presentation was actually good. Within ten minutes, her nervous system had shifted. Not because the problems disappeared. Because her brain had been redirected from what was missing to what was present. She slept. She delivered the presentation well. The gratitude didn't fix anything. It changed the lens she was using to see the situation, and that changed everything about how she showed up the next morning.

The daily gratitude ritual in this takeover is simple and takes less than three minutes. Every morning, before you start your day, write down three specific things you're grateful for. Not vague statements like "I'm grateful for my family." Specific ones. "I'm grateful that my manager gave me direct feedback yesterday, even though it was hard to hear, because it tells me exactly where to focus." "I'm grateful that I slept seven hours last night." "I'm grateful that I have a clear goal I'm working toward." The specificity is what makes it work. Vague gratitude is easy to dismiss. Specific gratitude requires you to actually look at your life and find what's genuinely there.

Do this for seven consecutive days. Don't skip a day because you're in a hurry or because you "don't feel grateful" right now. Especially don't skip it on the days you don't feel grateful. Those are the days the practice matters most. Gratitude isn't a record of how good your life is. It's a practice that trains your brain to find what's working even when things are hard. The harder the day, the more important it is to do the three minutes.

There's a second component to the gratitude practice that amplifies its effect. Once a day, share one thing you're grateful for with another person. Not in a forced or performative way. Just mention it naturally. "I was thinking today about how much I appreciate the way you handled that situation last week." "I'm really glad we have this team." "I wanted to tell you that the feedback you gave me made a real difference." Expressing gratitude out loud to another person does two things. It deepens the feeling in you, because articulating something makes it more real. And it creates a small but genuine moment of connection with the other person. Both of those outcomes are worth the thirty seconds it takes.

Gratitude also has a direct relationship with resilience, which is why it belongs in a chapter about mindset. Resilience isn't the absence of difficulty. It's the ability to move through difficulty without losing your footing. People who practice gratitude regularly tend to recover from setbacks faster, not because they're naive about what went wrong, but because they haven't lost sight of what's still intact. When you can hold both the difficulty and the good in view at the same time, you're less likely to catastrophize. Less likely to conclude that one bad outcome means everything is broken. That cognitive balance is what keeps you functional and forward-moving when the pressure is highest.

A grateful mindset and a growth mindset reinforce each other in a specific way. The growth mindset says that challenges are opportunities to learn. Gratitude says that even in a difficult situation, there's something worth noticing. Together, they create a mental environment where setbacks don't derail you and where progress, even slow progress, gets acknowledged and built upon. That combination is what makes the final weeks of this takeover sustainable. Not willpower. Not motivation. A trained mind that can find something to work with in almost any situation.

Start the gratitude practice today. Not tomorrow. Today. Write the three things right now, before you move to the next section. Make them specific. Say one of them out loud. That's the practice. Three minutes. Every day. For the rest of this phase and beyond.

Mindset is the ceiling on everything else you've built in this takeover. Your habits, your leadership, your self-security, your clarity about your values, all of it operates within the limits of what you believe is possible. A growth mindset raises that ceiling. Visualization and affirmation prime your nervous system to perform at the level you're working toward. Gratitude keeps your brain scanning for what's working rather than what's missing. These three tools aren't separate. They work as a system, and the system is most powerful when all three are running at the same time.

This week is day 64 through day 70 of your 98-day takeover. You're past the midpoint. The habits you've built are starting to compound. The identity work you've done is starting to show up in how you carry yourself. This is exactly the moment when your mindset either locks in the progress you've made or quietly starts to erode it. The three action steps below are designed to lock it in.

Action Step 1: Reframe one recent mistake as a specific lesson. Pick something that went wrong in the last two weeks. Not your biggest failure ever. Something recent and real. Write down exactly what happened in two sentences. Then write what you learned from it, specifically. Not "I learned to be more careful." Name the exact lesson. "I learned that I need to confirm the scope of a project in writing before I start the work." "I learned that I perform better when I prepare the night before rather than the morning of." That specific lesson is the data. Keep it. Use it. A mistake you've extracted a lesson from isn't a loss. It's an investment in the next attempt.

Action Step 2: Spend two minutes visualizing your goal as already achieved. Do this right now, before you move on. Sit quietly. Close your eyes. Take three slow breaths. Bring your current most important goal to mind and see it as complete. Use all five senses. What does the moment of completion look like? Sound like? Feel like in your body? Hold the image for ninety seconds with as much detail as you can generate. Then open your eyes and write one sentence about what that felt like. Then write one action you'll take today toward that goal. Do the action.

Action Step 3: Write down three things you are grateful for right now. Open your journal. Write today's date. Write three specific things, not general ones, that you're genuinely grateful for at this moment. Make each one at least one full sentence. Then say one of them out loud. Then share one of them with another person before the day ends, in whatever way feels natural. That's the complete practice. Three minutes. Do it again tomorrow morning. And the morning after that.

These three steps don't require extra time you don't have. They require about ten minutes total. What they do require is that you actually do them rather than reading about them and moving on. The mindset work in this phase only becomes real through the practice. The practice only becomes powerful through consistency. And consistency, as you've learned across every phase of this takeover, is the one thing that turns insight into identity.

The superior self you're building isn't just someone with better habits or clearer goals. It's someone whose mind works for them rather than against them. Someone who sees a setback and asks what it's teaching them. Someone who walks into a high-stakes moment having already rehearsed it in their mind. Someone who starts each day by deliberately noticing what's worth building on. That person isn't a distant aspiration. They're the version of you that shows up when these three practices are running consistently. You already have everything you need to be that person. You just have to do the work.

Phase 11: Building Resilience and Grit

You're at day 71. The habits are forming. The mindset work is settling in. And right now, something real is happening inside you, something that the early phases of this takeover couldn't have produced. You're starting to feel the weight of sustained effort. The novelty is long gone. The motivation you felt on day one is no longer carrying you. What's carrying you now is something different. Something harder to name but more durable. That something is what this entire phase is about.

Resilience and grit aren't the same thing, though they work together. Resilience is your ability to absorb a hit and come back stronger. Grit is your willingness to keep showing up when nothing is hitting you, when it's just the ordinary grind of doing the work day after day without applause, without visible results, without any guarantee that it's going to pay off. Both of them matter. And both of them can be built deliberately, which is exactly what the next seven days of this takeover are designed to do.

Most people treat resilience like a personality trait. You either have it or you don't. That framing is wrong, and it's worth saying clearly. Resilience is a skill. It's built through specific practices, specific ways of thinking about setbacks, and specific habits of emotional regulation that you develop over time. The same is true for grit. It's not a fixed quantity you were born with. It's a capacity that grows through use, through the repeated experience of pushing through difficulty and discovering that you can.

Everything you've built in the previous ten phases of this takeover has been preparing you for this. The self-awareness from Phase 2 is what lets you catch your own reactions before they derail you. The identity work from Phase 3 gives you a stable sense of self to return to when things get hard. The values clarity from Phase 5 tells you what's worth fighting for. The habit systems from Phase 9 keep you moving even when motivation is gone. Resilience and grit aren't separate from all of that. They're the expression of all of it under pressure.

The Resilience Advantage

Resilience isn't about being tough in the way people usually mean that word. It's not about suppressing your emotions or pretending setbacks don't hurt. Real resilience is more honest than that. It means you feel the hit, you process what happened, and then you make a deliberate choice about where to go from there. The key word is deliberate. That's what separates resilience from just surviving.

Think about what actually happens when something goes wrong. A project falls apart. A relationship hits a wall. A goal you've been working toward doesn't materialize the way you expected. For most people, the initial reaction is some version of the same sequence: shock, then frustration, then a story. And the story is usually the most dangerous part. Because the story you tell yourself about what happened determines whether the setback becomes a detour or a dead end.

Consider a hypothetical scenario: imagine someone like Simone, a 34-year-old brand strategist who pitched a major client for three months, built the entire proposal around her firm's strongest capabilities, and lost the contract to a competitor at the final stage. The loss was real and it stung. Her first instinct was to conclude that she wasn't good enough at pitching, that her firm was behind the curve, that maybe she'd been overestimating her own abilities. She sat with those thoughts for two days. Then she did something that changed the outcome of the next six months. She wrote down every assumption she'd made during the pitch process and asked herself which ones had actually been tested and which ones she'd just believed. She found three specific places where she'd made guesses instead of asking direct questions about what the client actually needed. The loss wasn't about her talent. It was about a gap in her process. That distinction, between a verdict on her worth and a specific, fixable gap in her approach, is exactly what resilience looks like in practice. She came back to the next pitch with a better process and won.

Managing your emotional reaction to stress is the first layer of building resilience, and it starts with your body. Before your thinking brain has processed what's happening, your nervous system has already responded. Your heart rate goes up. Your muscles tighten. Your thinking narrows. That's not weakness. That's biology. The question isn't whether your body responds to stress. It's whether you let that initial response make your decisions for you.

The three-breath pause you've been using since Phase 2 is your most immediate tool here. When something goes wrong, when a trigger fires, when the pressure spikes, stop before you react. Three slow breaths, four counts in, six counts out. That sequence activates your parasympathetic nervous system and starts to bring your prefrontal cortex back online. You're not suppressing the reaction. You're creating the gap between the feeling and the response. That gap is where your resilience actually lives.

Perspective is the second layer. When you're inside a crisis, it always feels larger than it actually is. That's not a character flaw. It's a feature of how the brain processes threat. The problem is that a brain in threat mode makes worse decisions, sees fewer options, and catastrophizes more readily. Perspective is the deliberate act of zooming out. Asking yourself: will this matter in six months? What's actually within my control right now? What's the most useful thing I can do in the next twenty-four hours? These questions don't minimize what happened. They redirect your attention from the part you can't control to the part you can.

Emotional resilience also involves your inner dialogue during hard times. The self-talk audit from Phase 2 is directly relevant here. When a setback hits, your inner critic often gets louder. It uses the difficulty as evidence for the limiting beliefs you've been working to dismantle. "See? I knew this wouldn't work." "This always happens to me." "I'm not cut out for this." These thoughts feel like honest assessments. They're not. They're the fixed mindset showing up under pressure, which is exactly when it's most convincing and most dangerous.

Catch the thought. Name it. Then ask whether it's actually true or whether it just feels true right now. Most of the time, under stress, your inner critic is running a distortion, not a diagnosis. The reframe you built in Phase 10 applies here too. "This always happens to me" becomes "this is a hard situation that I'm going to work through." "I'm not cut out for this" becomes "I haven't solved this yet, and I'm figuring out how." The new statement doesn't have to feel completely true in the moment. It just has to be more accurate than the catastrophe the inner critic is selling.

Adaptability is one of the most underrated components of resilience, and it deserves its own attention. The people who recover from setbacks fastest aren't always the ones with the most talent or the most resources. They're the ones who adjust the quickest. They don't spend weeks insisting the situation should be different from what it is. They assess what's actually in front of them and start working with that instead of against it.

Adaptability doesn't mean abandoning your goals when things get hard. It means being flexible about the path while staying committed to the destination. If the road you planned is blocked, you don't stop moving. You find a different road. That requires a specific kind of mental flexibility, the ability to hold your goal firmly while holding your method loosely. Most people get this backwards. They cling to the method and let the goal drift. Resilient people do the opposite.

Here's a specific practice for building adaptability right now. Think about one current obstacle in your life, something that's blocking your progress on a goal that matters to you. Write it down in one sentence. Then write three completely different ways you could approach it. Not variations of the same approach. Three genuinely different angles. One of them might feel obvious. Push past it. The second one might feel uncomfortable. Write it anyway. The third might feel unlikely. Write it regardless. The point isn't to find the perfect solution. The point is to train your brain to generate options rather than getting locked onto a single path. A brain that can generate options is a resilient brain. A brain that can only see one way forward is a fragile one.

Support systems are the final layer of resilience that most people undervalue until they need them. You can't build resilience entirely in isolation. Human beings are wired for connection, and the research on this is consistent: people with strong social support recover from setbacks faster, experience less chronic stress, and maintain better physical and mental health over time. This isn't about having people around who tell you everything is fine. It's about having people who can offer honest perspective, genuine encouragement, and practical help when you actually need it.

Look at your current support system honestly. Not the people you talk to casually, but the people you could actually call when something goes wrong. The ones who'd tell you the truth rather than just what you want to hear. The ones whose perspective genuinely helps you see more clearly. If that list is short, building it is part of your resilience work. It's not a nice-to-have. It's infrastructure.

Reach out to one person in your support system this week, not because something is wrong, but specifically to check in. Tell them you're doing resilience work as part of your takeover and ask them one direct question: "When you've seen me at my best under pressure, what have you noticed about how I handle it?" Their answer will tell you something about your existing strengths that you might not be able to see from the inside. And the act of reaching out, before you're in crisis, strengthens the connection so it's there when you actually need it.

Grit and Perseverance

Grit is the quality that separates the people who start from the people who finish. That's not a dramatic statement. It's just accurate. The world is full of people who are talented, motivated, and genuinely committed to changing their lives, right up until the point where the work stops being interesting and starts being just work. That's the moment grit either shows up or it doesn't.

The "dip" is what that moment feels like from the inside. You've been working toward something for a while. The initial excitement is gone. You're not seeing the results you expected yet. The effort feels high and the reward feels distant. Everything in you wants to either quit or pivot to something new, something that still has that early-stage energy. This is the moment most people leave. And it's also, if you stay, the moment everything starts to compound.

The dip isn't a sign that you chose wrong. It's a sign that you're deep enough into something for it to start being real. The early stages of anything are energized by novelty. The middle stages are where you find out whether you actually want this or whether you just wanted the idea of it. The people who get through the dip aren't the ones who feel more motivated than everyone else. They're the ones who've built a system that doesn't require motivation to function.

That's what you've been building since Phase 9. Your habit stacks, your accountability structure, your Visual Progress Map, these aren't just organizational tools. They're your grit infrastructure. When motivation is gone and discipline alone feels thin, the system carries you. You don't have to decide every morning whether to show up. The decision was already made when you built the system. You just follow it.

Think about a hypothetical scenario: imagine someone like Derek, a 29-year-old software developer who started this takeover with a clear goal: to build enough discipline and self-awareness to finally launch the side project he'd been "about to start" for two years. For the first four weeks, he was consistent. Then week five hit. Work got heavier. He missed two days of his morning routine. By week six, he'd told himself he'd restart "when things calmed down." He recognized the pattern, though, because he'd been tracking it on his Visual Progress Map. He could see exactly when the drift started and how fast it accelerated. That visibility was the intervention. He didn't wait for things to calm down. He did a five-minute version of his routine the next morning, just enough to break the gap. Then ten minutes the morning after. By day three he was back to the full routine. The grit wasn't in the willpower to push through. It was in the system that made the return path short enough to actually take.

Effort over the long haul requires something that motivation can't provide: a reason that doesn't depend on how you feel. Your values, the ones you named and ranked in Phase 5, are that reason. When you're in the dip and everything in you wants to stop, going back to your non-negotiables gives you something solid to stand on. Not "I feel like doing this today" but "this aligns with what I've said matters most to me, and I'm not willing to compromise that." That's a different kind of fuel. It burns slower and it lasts longer.

There's also a specific mental technique for pushing through the dip that's worth building into your practice. It's called the five-minute rule, and it works like this. When you're avoiding a task or a practice because the resistance feels too high, you commit to doing it for exactly five minutes. Not the full thing. Five minutes. Set a timer. Start. Most of the time, once you're in motion, the resistance drops and you continue past the five minutes naturally. The hardest part of almost any difficult task is the first thirty seconds. The five-minute rule gets you through those thirty seconds by making the commitment small enough that your brain stops treating it as a threat.

If you do stop at five minutes, that's fine too. You showed up. You did something. You kept the chain going. Showing up imperfectly is always better than not showing up at all, because showing up maintains the identity of someone who follows through. Not showing up starts to build the identity of someone who doesn't. Over 98 days, those two identities look completely different from each other.

Self-doubt during the dip is almost universal. When you're not seeing results yet and the effort is high, the inner critic gets very busy. "Maybe this isn't working." "Maybe I'm not the kind of person who can do this." "Maybe I should try a different approach." These thoughts sound like reasonable self-assessment. In the dip, they're almost never that. They're the resistance talking. The way to test whether a thought is genuine useful feedback or just resistance is to ask: am I thinking this because I have new information that suggests I should change course, or am I thinking this because I'm tired and uncomfortable? If it's the second one, the answer is to keep going, not to pivot.

Rewriting your internal narrative during the dip is one of the most powerful things you can do. The story you tell yourself about where you are in the process determines whether the dip feels like failure or like a necessary part of the path. "I'm falling behind" is a story. "I'm in the hard middle, which is exactly where progress happens" is a different story. Both are responses to the same facts. Only one of them keeps you moving.

Write your current dip story down. The honest version, whatever you've been telling yourself about where you are right now. Then rewrite it using the growth mindset lens from Phase 10. Not a fantasy. A more accurate version that acknowledges the difficulty without concluding that it means something permanent. Read the rewritten version out loud. Then do the next thing your system asks you to do. That's grit. Not a feeling. A sequence of decisions made in spite of the feeling.

Grit also has a social dimension that's easy to miss. The people you're around during the hard stretches either reinforce your commitment or quietly erode it. Someone who consistently normalizes quitting, who treats the dip as evidence that something isn't working, will make it harder for you to stay the course. Someone who holds you accountable with honesty and warmth will make it easier. This is one more reason why the support system work from the previous section isn't optional. Your environment shapes your behavior more than your willpower does. Build the environment that makes grit easier to sustain.

Learning from Failure

Failure is a data point. Not a verdict. Not a destination. A data point. That reframe sounds simple, but it changes everything about how you move through setbacks when you actually hold it.

Most people treat failure as evidence about who they are. A failed project means they're not capable enough. A missed goal means they don't have what it takes. A mistake in a high-stakes moment means they'll always crack under pressure. These conclusions feel like honest self-assessment. They're not. They're the fixed mindset doing what it always does: turning a specific, temporary event into a permanent statement about character. The event was real. The conclusion is invented.

Failure as data means something specific. It means every setback contains information you didn't have before. About what didn't work. About what assumption was wrong. About what gap in your preparation or your process the outcome exposed. That information is genuinely valuable, but only if you extract it deliberately. Most people don't. They feel the sting of failure, they move away from it as fast as possible, and they never actually mine it for what it's worth. Then they're surprised when the same pattern shows up again.

The failure deconstruction process is a four-step practice you apply every time something significant doesn't go the way you planned. It takes about fifteen minutes and it turns a painful experience into a practical asset.

Step one is to describe what happened without interpretation. Write a factual account of the event in two to three sentences. Not "I completely bombed the presentation." The facts: "I presented to the client on Thursday. I lost the thread of my argument in the second section. The client asked several clarifying questions I wasn't prepared for." Just the facts. No story yet. This step is harder than it sounds because the brain immediately wants to add meaning. Resist that for now.

Step two is to identify the specific gap. Ask yourself: what was the distance between what I expected to happen and what actually happened? Then ask: what contributed to that gap? Not who caused it. What contributed to it. This keeps the analysis useful rather than defensive. You're looking for the actual mechanism of the failure, not a place to assign blame. Was it a preparation gap? A communication gap? A skills gap? A planning gap? An assumption that turned out to be wrong? Name it specifically. "I assumed the client already understood the context behind the recommendation. They didn't. I hadn't built in time to establish that context."

Step three is to extract the lesson. Ask yourself: if I were going to face a similar situation again, what would I do differently based on what I now know? Write the answer as a specific, actionable statement. Not "I'd be better prepared." What does better prepared actually look like? "I'd spend fifteen minutes before any client presentation confirming what they already understand about the context, so I know exactly where to start." That's a lesson you can actually use. Vague lessons evaporate. Specific ones stick.

Step four is to decide on one concrete change. Based on the lesson you just wrote, what's one thing you'll do differently starting now? Not a list of ten improvements. One change. The most important one. Write it down. Then put it somewhere you'll see it before the next similar situation arises. That's the lesson converted into action, which is the only form of a lesson that actually prevents the same mistake from happening again.

Ownership is the mindset that makes this process work. You can only extract value from a failure you're willing to own. If your default response to things going wrong is to look for external causes, the weather, the timing, the other person's behavior, you'll never get the information that's actually available to you. That's not to say external factors don't exist. They do. But external factors are outside your control. Your preparation, your process, your assumptions, your communication, these are within your control. And they're where the most useful lessons live.

Blame keeps you stuck. Taking responsibility sets you free. Not because it feels better in the moment, it usually doesn't. But because responsibility gives you agency. If the failure was caused by something outside you, there's nothing you can do about it. If it was caused by something within your process, you can fix it. Ownership is the choice to focus on the part you can actually change.

Feedback from other people is one of the most valuable and most underused sources of failure data available to you. When something goes wrong, the people who were there often see things you couldn't see from the inside. Your blind spots are invisible to you by definition. Other people can see them. Asking for honest feedback after a setback isn't weakness. It's intelligence. It's using every available data source to understand what happened as completely as possible.

The practice here is specific. After a significant setback, identify one person who was close enough to the situation to have useful perspective. Ask them one direct question: "What did you observe that I might not have seen from where I was standing?" Then listen without defending. You don't have to agree with everything they say. You don't have to take every observation as final truth. But you do have to actually hear it before you decide what to do with it. The moment you get defensive, you close the data stream. Stay open. The discomfort of honest feedback is always less costly than the blind spot it reveals.

Failure also has a relationship with identity that's worth naming directly. When you've done the identity work in Phase 3, when you know who you are at your core independent of your results, failure stops being existentially threatening. It stops feeling like a verdict on your worth. It becomes what it actually is: information about a specific attempt in a specific situation. You are not your last result. You are the person who learns from results and keeps moving. That distinction, felt deeply rather than just understood intellectually, is what allows you to fail without being diminished by it.

You've already proven you can do hard things. Every phase of this takeover that you've worked through is evidence of that. The failures you encounter in the remaining weeks aren't interruptions to your growth. They're part of it. They're where the most important learning happens, if you're willing to stay present with them long enough to extract what they're offering.

Your Next Move

Grit is the differentiator between the people who start and the people who finish. You've started. You're in week eleven of a fourteen-week takeover, and you're still here. That's not nothing. That's already evidence of something real being built inside you.

The work of this phase doesn't end when you close this chapter. It continues in every moment over the coming days when the resistance shows up and you choose to keep moving anyway. In every setback you encounter and choose to mine for data rather than run from. In every dip you push through not because you feel motivated but because the system holds you and your values point you forward.

Three specific actions to take before you move into Phase 12.

Action Step 1: Identify your current obstacle and map three ways to adapt. Open your journal right now. Write down the single biggest obstacle you're facing in your life or in this takeover at this moment. Be specific. One sentence. Then write three genuinely different approaches to that obstacle. Not variations on the same idea. Three different angles. For each one, write one concrete first action you could take within 48 hours. You don't have to commit to all three paths. You just have to see that options exist. A brain that can see three paths is significantly more resilient than one that can only see one or none. Choose the approach that feels most aligned with your values and take the first action on it before tomorrow ends.

Action Step 2: Reach out to your support system for a resilience check-in. Identify one person in your life who knows you well enough to give you honest perspective. Contact them today, by message, call, or in person. Tell them you're working on building resilience and you'd value their honest input. Ask them this specific question: "When you've seen me handle something difficult well, what did you notice about how I approached it?" Then ask a second question: "Is there anything you've observed that you think might be getting in my way right now?" Listen without defending. Write down what they say. You don't have to act on all of it, but you do have to genuinely hear it. The perspective of someone who cares about you and can see you clearly is one of the most valuable inputs available to you. Use it.

Action Step 3: Commit to one difficult task you've been avoiding. There's something on your list that you've been circling around. You know what it is. The task that keeps getting moved to tomorrow. The conversation you haven't had. The decision you haven't made. The project you haven't started. Write it down right now. Then write why you've been avoiding it. Be honest. Is it fear of failure? Fear of the effort involved? Uncertainty about the outcome? Name the actual reason. Then apply the five-minute rule. Commit to working on this task for exactly five minutes today. Set the timer. Start. That's it. Five minutes. The act of starting breaks the avoidance loop. What happens after the five minutes is up to you, but the starting is non-negotiable. Do it today, not tomorrow. Today is the only day that actually exists right now, and the version of yourself you're building through this takeover shows up today, not someday.

Resilience and grit aren't qualities you either have or don't have. They're capacities you've been building, day by day, through every phase of this takeover. The self-awareness that lets you catch your reactions before they derail you. The identity that stays stable when results are uncertain. The values that give you a reason to keep going that doesn't depend on how you feel. The habits that carry you through the dip. The mindset that turns failure into fuel. All of it has been pointing here, to this phase, to this week, to this moment where the work gets real and the person you're becoming either shows up or doesn't. They're showing up. Keep going.

Phase 12: Purpose, Passion, and Calling

You've made it to week twelve. That's not a small thing. You've built habits, examined your identity, clarified your values, developed your leadership, and pushed through the dip when everything in you wanted to stop. All of that work was real. And now it points toward the question that sits underneath everything else you've been doing for the past eleven weeks. Not "what do I do?" or "how do I do it better?" but something deeper and more fundamental than either of those. The question is: why does any of it matter to you?

That question is what Phase 12 is about.

Purpose, passion, and calling aren't soft concepts reserved for people who have the luxury of thinking about meaning. They're the engine underneath everything else. When your daily work connects to something you genuinely care about, something that feels larger than a paycheck or a title, everything changes. Your resilience gets stronger because you have a real reason to push through. Your habits stick because they're feeding something that matters. Your leadership deepens because you're not just managing tasks, you're contributing to something worth contributing to. The B.O.S.S. takeover has been building toward this from day one.

This week, you're going to get specific about your why.

Discovering Your 'Why'

Most people can tell you what they do. A smaller number can tell you how they do it well. Very few can tell you, with any real clarity, why they do it at all. Not the practical answer, not "because I need the money" or "because I'm good at it," but the actual reason. The one that gets you out of bed when nothing else would. The one that makes the hard days feel worth it.

That's your why. And finding it starts with understanding the difference between a job, a career, and a calling.

A job is a transaction. You show up, you do the work, you get paid. There's nothing wrong with that. It's honest and it's necessary. But a job, on its own, doesn't provide the kind of deep satisfaction that makes a person feel genuinely alive in what they do. It's a means to an end, and most people know it. They feel it every Sunday evening when the low-level dread starts to build.

A career is something more than a job. It's a progression, a direction, a sequence of roles and experiences that build on each other over time. People with careers feel a sense of investment in where they're going. They think about growth, advancement, and development. That's meaningful. But a career alone can still leave a gap. You can climb a ladder for twenty years and reach the top only to realize it was leaning against the wrong wall.

A calling is different from both. A calling is the sense that what you're doing isn't just what you're good at or what you've been trained for. It's what you're meant to contribute. It's the intersection of your deepest strengths, your genuine passions, and a need in the world that you're uniquely positioned to meet. When you're working in your calling, the work doesn't feel like performance. It feels like expression. It feels like you're being exactly who you're supposed to be, doing exactly what you're supposed to do. That feeling is rare. But it's real, and it's available to you.

The path from job to calling isn't always dramatic. It doesn't always require you to quit everything and start over. For some people, discovering their calling means completely redesigning their professional life. For others, it means finding ways to bring more of their real purpose into the work they're already doing. Both are valid. What matters is that you stop drifting and start choosing.

Think about someone like Andre, a hypothetical 41-year-old operations director who had spent fifteen years building an impressive career in logistics. He was respected, well-compensated, and genuinely good at his work. But something had been missing for years, something he couldn't quite name. When he started this kind of purpose work, he traced it back to a pattern he'd never paid attention to before. The moments in his career that felt most alive weren't the big contract wins or the promotions. They were the moments he spent mentoring younger team members, helping them see their own potential and develop their skills. He'd always treated that as a side activity, something he did because he cared about people, not something that counted as real work. When he finally named it clearly, he realized his calling wasn't logistics. It was developing people. Logistics was just the context. That realization didn't make him quit his job the next day. But it changed how he spent his energy within it, and it opened a door to a path he'd never seriously considered before.

Passion is the fuel that drives you toward your calling. Purpose is the direction that fuel points you in. These two things work together in a way that's worth understanding clearly. Passion without purpose can feel exciting but scattered, lots of energy with no clear destination. Purpose without passion can feel meaningful but exhausting, the right direction but no fuel to sustain the journey. When the two connect, when what you love doing also serves something larger than yourself, that's when the energy becomes genuinely self-sustaining. You stop needing to manufacture motivation because the work itself provides it.

Discovering your why starts with honest self-examination, the same kind you've been practicing throughout this takeover. But now you're applying it to the deepest layer. Not "what am I good at?" but "what do I care about enough to give my best energy to?" Not "what have I been trained to do?" but "what would I do even if no one was watching and no one was paying me?"

There's a specific exercise for this called the Deathbed Test, and it's worth doing right now. It sounds dramatic, but it's one of the most clarifying things you can do. Close your eyes for a moment and imagine yourself at the very end of a long, full life. You're looking back at everything. The question isn't "what did I achieve?" The question is: "what mattered?" What do you hope you spent your time on? What do you hope you contributed? What do you hope people felt because you were in their lives? Write down what comes up. Don't filter it. Don't make it sound impressive. Just write what actually moves you when you sit with that question honestly.

What you write is a map to your purpose.

Fear is almost always present in this conversation. The fear that what you actually care about isn't practical. The fear that it's too late to pursue it. The fear that naming it out loud makes you accountable to it in a way that feels terrifying. These fears are real, and they're worth acknowledging. But they're also familiar by now. You've worked with fear throughout this takeover. You know it's a signal, not a verdict. The fact that something scares you is often the clearest sign that it actually matters to you. Things that don't matter don't scare you. They just don't interest you.

Overcoming obstacles to purpose isn't about eliminating the fear. It's about moving forward in spite of it. The self-doubt you might feel when you try to name your calling isn't proof that you don't have one. It's proof that you're getting close to something real. Stay with it. The clarity you're looking for doesn't always arrive all at once. Sometimes it comes in pieces, one honest reflection at a time.

Your purpose doesn't have to be a single grand mission. For most people, it's simpler and more personal than that. It might be to help people feel less alone. To build things that last. To teach what you know. To create beauty. To solve problems that others overlook. To lead in a way that brings out the best in the people around you. These aren't small purposes. They're the ones that quietly shape everything you do when you're at your best.

Start here. Write one sentence that begins with the words: "I am here to..." Don't overthink it. Don't try to make it perfect. Write the first honest thing that comes up. That sentence is your starting point. It doesn't have to be final. It just has to be true right now. You can refine it as you go. But you can't build on something that doesn't exist yet.

Aligning Work and Purpose

Knowing your purpose is one thing. Bringing it into your actual daily work is something else entirely. Most people assume that aligning work and purpose requires a dramatic change, a career pivot, a new business, a complete reinvention. Sometimes that's true. But more often, the alignment starts much smaller than that. It starts with a shift in how you see what you're already doing.

Every job, no matter how routine it might feel, has a ripple effect. Every role touches other people in some way. The question isn't whether your work contributes to something. It does. The question is whether you're conscious of that contribution and whether you're making it in a way that reflects what you actually care about.

Think about a hypothetical scenario: imagine someone like Camille, a 29-year-old customer service manager at a mid-sized software company. She was good at her job and genuinely liked her team, but she'd been feeling disconnected from the work for about a year. She told herself that customer service wasn't exactly a calling. It was just a job she was good at. When she did this purpose work, she realized that what she cared about most was helping people feel heard and respected, especially when they were frustrated or overwhelmed. She looked at her daily work through that lens and saw it completely differently. Every difficult call was an opportunity to do exactly that. Every time she trained a team member to handle a complaint with patience and genuine care, she was living out her purpose. Nothing about her job description changed. Everything about how she showed up in it did. Within six months, her team's satisfaction scores had climbed significantly, and she'd been asked to lead the company's customer experience redesign. The work hadn't changed. She had.

Bringing your values and passions into your current professional environment doesn't require permission. It requires intention. It requires you to stop waiting for the perfect role to show up and start looking for the places where your real strengths and genuine care can show up in the role you already have.

There are three specific strategies for doing this, and they work at different levels depending on where you are in your career.

The first strategy is purpose reframing. This means consciously connecting your daily tasks to the larger impact they create. When you're doing work that feels routine or disconnected, ask yourself: who benefits from this? How does this contribute to something that matters? The answer doesn't have to be grand. A financial analyst who frames their work as "helping the organization make decisions that protect people's jobs" is doing the same work as one who sees it as "running numbers." The difference in energy and engagement is significant.

The second strategy is strength activation. Look at your current role and identify the three tasks or responsibilities that most naturally draw on your deepest strengths. The ones from your ten core qualities list in Phase 3. Now ask: how can you do more of those? Can you volunteer for projects that require those strengths? Can you restructure how you approach your current work to lean more heavily on what you do best? You won't always be able to eliminate the tasks that drain you. But you can often increase the proportion of your time spent on the ones that energize you, and that shift matters more than most people realize.

The third strategy is contribution mapping. This is the practice of deliberately identifying how your work serves other people. Not in a vague, theoretical way. Specifically. Write down three people or groups who are directly affected by the work you do. Then write one specific way your work makes their lives better, easier, or more meaningful. This exercise does something important. It moves your focus from what you're producing to who you're serving. And service, when it's genuine, is one of the most reliable sources of purpose available to anyone.

Values alignment is the foundation under all three of these strategies. When the way you spend your time reflects what you actually believe in, something settles. You feel more coherent. More whole. Less like you're performing a role and more like you're expressing who you actually are. When there's a significant gap between your values and your daily work, that gap doesn't stay quiet. It shows up as the low-level resentment, the Sunday dread, the hollow feeling that something is missing even when everything looks fine from the outside.

If you've done your values work from Phase 5 honestly, you already know what your non-negotiables are. Now the question is: how well does your current work honor them? Not perfectly. That's rarely possible. But enough. Enough that the work feels like an expression of who you are rather than a contradiction of it. If the gap is too wide, that's important information. Not a reason to panic, but a signal worth taking seriously. Sometimes the answer is to find ways to bring more of your values into your current context. Sometimes the answer is that the context itself needs to change. Either way, naming the gap clearly is the first step toward doing something about it.

Joy in the process is something worth addressing directly, because a lot of people who are working toward a larger purpose forget to find satisfaction in the daily work that gets them there. They're so focused on the destination that they miss the fact that the path itself is where most of their life actually happens. If you're going to spend forty or fifty hours a week doing something, the quality of that experience matters. Not just the outcome.

Finding joy in the process doesn't mean pretending everything is enjoyable. Some tasks are just tasks. But it does mean looking for the moments within your daily work that genuinely engage you, that make you feel alive and capable and connected to something real. Those moments are always there if you're looking for them. The conversation with a colleague that sparks a new idea. The problem that finally cracks after you've been working on it for days. The moment someone you've been helping finally gets it. These moments aren't bonuses. They're the substance of a life lived with purpose.

Pay attention to them. Write them down. Let them remind you, especially on the hard days, that what you're doing matters. Not because someone told you it does. Because you've seen it with your own eyes, in the small moments that add up to something real over time.

Passion in daily life is about weaving what energizes you into the fabric of what you do, not saving it for some future version of your life that has more time and fewer obligations. You don't need a perfect setup to start living with more purpose. You need fifteen minutes a day and the willingness to pay attention to what actually lights you up.

Go back to your Flow Inventory from Phase 6. Look at the three activities you circled, the ones that felt most alive. Now ask yourself one honest question: is there any version of my current daily life that could include more of these? Not all of them. Not perfectly. Just more. A small increase in how much of your day involves something you genuinely care about changes the entire texture of the day. Over weeks and months, it changes the entire texture of your life.

A calling isn't something that happens to you. It's something you build, day by day, through the choices you make about where to put your energy and attention. The 98-Day Superior Self Takeover has been giving you the tools to make those choices deliberately. This week is where you use those tools to answer the deepest question the takeover asks: not what are you doing, but what are you here for?

That answer is worth everything it takes to find it.

Putting It Into Practice

A life lived with purpose is the destination this entire takeover has been pointing toward. Not a perfect life. Not a life without difficulty or uncertainty. A life where what you do on a daily basis connects to something you genuinely care about, where your work reflects your values, and where the contribution you make to the world around you is intentional rather than accidental. That's the superior self the B.O.S.S. takeover is designed to help you become.

The three actions below are the most important ones in this entire book. Not because they're the most complex. Because they're the ones that bring everything else together. Every phase you've worked through, every habit you've built, every belief you've examined, every value you've named, it all feeds into what you're about to do right now.

Don't rush these. Give each one the time and honesty it deserves.

Action Step 1: Write a purpose statement for your current role. This is not a job description. It's a statement of why your role exists and what it makes possible for the people it touches. Start with the formula: "My purpose in this role is to [what you do] so that [who benefits] can [what becomes possible for them]." A teacher might write: "My purpose in this role is to create a space where students feel safe enough to think for themselves, so that they can build the confidence to solve problems the world hasn't invented yet." A project manager might write: "My purpose in this role is to remove the friction between talented people and the work they're capable of, so that the team can do their best work without getting lost in the process." Write yours. Make it specific to you, your actual role, and the real people your work affects. Read it out loud when you're done. If it doesn't move you even slightly, it's not specific enough yet. Rewrite it until it does.

Action Step 2: Identify one specific way your work contributes to others. Not a general statement. One concrete, specific example. Think about one person, a colleague, a client, a customer, a team member, even a family member who benefits from what you do. Write their name or their role. Then write exactly how your work makes their life better, easier, or more meaningful. One sentence. "Because I do my job well, [this person] gets to [this specific benefit]." That sentence is your contribution made visible. Read it when the work feels hollow. Read it when you're questioning whether any of it matters. It matters. You've just written down exactly how.

Action Step 3: Do one passionate action today that connects to your calling. Not tomorrow. Today. Before this day ends. It doesn't have to be grand. It has to be genuine. Pick one activity that connects to what you identified as your calling or your deepest passion. Spend at least thirty minutes on it, fully present, without multitasking. If your calling involves teaching, teach something to someone today. If it involves creating, create something. If it involves helping, find one person to help in a specific and meaningful way. If it involves building, start building something, even just the first small piece. The point isn't the output. The point is the experience of doing something that actually matters to you, on purpose, today. That experience is what you're building your life around. Give it thirty minutes and see what it tells you about where you're supposed to be going.

These three actions together take about an hour. That hour is the most important one you'll spend this week. Not because it solves everything, but because it starts something. It turns the purpose work you've been doing throughout this takeover from a concept into a practice. And practice, done consistently over the remaining days of this 98-day commitment and beyond, is what transforms a life that's been running on default into one that's been designed with intention.

You started this takeover because something in you knew that where you were wasn't where you were supposed to stay. Twelve phases later, you have the self-awareness to see yourself clearly, the habits to show up consistently, the mindset to keep going when it's hard, and now the purpose to make all of it mean something. That combination is rare. It's also exactly what the superior self you've been building looks like from the inside.

Phase 13: Empowering Relationships and Communication

No matter how much inner work you do, how sharp your habits get, or how clear your purpose becomes, you don't live your life in isolation. You live it in rooms full of other people. At the conference table. Around the dinner table. In the car, in the hallway, on the phone, in the group chat. The quality of those interactions, day after day, shapes your experience of everything else you've built through this takeover.

That's the truth most personal development systems quietly skip over. They focus on the individual and treat relationships as a side effect. But relationships aren't a side effect. They're the environment your growth either thrives or suffocates in. The habits you've built, the mindset you've developed, the purpose you've named, all of it gets tested and expressed through the people around you. Not in a vacuum. Not in a journal. In real conversations, with real people, in real time.

Week thirteen is about that reality.

You're at day 85 of 98. You've done the hardest internal work this takeover asks of you. Now the focus shifts outward, not away from yourself, but through yourself and into the relationships that make up your actual life. The communication patterns you run. The boundaries you hold or don't hold. The conflicts you navigate or avoid. The people you spend your energy on and what that's doing to your growth. These aren't peripheral concerns. They're central to everything the 98-Day Superior Self Takeover is building toward.

The Power of Connection

Connection is the part of human life that most people underinvest in until something breaks. They're busy. They're focused. They have goals to hit and habits to maintain and a takeover to finish. Relationships get scheduled in the margins, squeezed between everything that feels more urgent. And then one day they look up and realize that their calendar is full but their life feels empty. That hollowness has a name. It's disconnection.

Real connection isn't about the number of people you know. It's not about your LinkedIn network or how many people show up at your birthday. It's about the quality of the bonds you actually have. The relationships where you can be honest without performing. Where you're known, not just recognized. Where you can bring the real version of yourself, the uncertain, still-figuring-it-out version, and have that version be genuinely welcomed.

Those relationships don't form by accident. They form through consistent, intentional presence. Through showing up not just when things are good, but when they're hard. Through listening in a way that makes the other person feel like what they're saying actually matters to you. Through being willing to be seen, not just to be impressive.

Think about a hypothetical scenario: imagine someone like Nia, a 34-year-old marketing manager who had a full social life on paper. She had colleagues she liked, a solid friend group, family she stayed in touch with. But when her father had a health scare and she found herself sitting in a hospital waiting room, she realized she didn't know who to call. Not because no one cared about her, but because she'd never let anyone in far enough to know when she actually needed them. She'd been excellent at being present for other people's hard moments. She'd never let anyone be present for hers. The connection she'd been building for years was real, but it was one-directional. She'd been giving without receiving, and that imbalance had left her more alone than her calendar suggested.

The first step toward deeper connection isn't finding new people. It's showing up differently with the ones you already have. That means being honest about what you're actually experiencing instead of defaulting to "I'm fine." It means asking real questions instead of small talk. It means being present in a conversation instead of half-there while your mind runs through your to-do list. These shifts are small in action and significant in impact.

Here's your specific practice for this section. In your next three social interactions, whether professional or personal, commit to one thing: full presence. Before the conversation starts, put your phone away or face down. Make eye contact. Ask one question that goes deeper than the surface. Something like: "What's been the hardest part of your week?" or "What are you most focused on right now?" Then actually listen to the answer. Don't plan your response while they're talking. Just take in what they're saying. Notice what shifts in the quality of the interaction when you're genuinely there for it.

Support and encouragement are a two-way street. You've been building the capacity to show up for yourself throughout this takeover. Now you're building the capacity to show up for others, and to actually let them show up for you. Both directions matter. A person who only gives becomes depleted. A person who only receives becomes isolated. Real connection requires both.

Belonging, the felt sense that you are part of something and that your presence in it matters, is one of the deepest human needs. It's not a luxury. When it's absent, everything else gets harder. Your resilience drops. Your motivation thins. Your sense of purpose feels more abstract and less real. When it's present, the opposite happens. You feel more capable, more grounded, more willing to take risks because you know there's something to come back to. Building that sense of belonging, in your workplace, your community, your personal life, is part of what it means to design a superior life rather than just a successful one.

Communication with Purpose

Most people think they're good communicators. Most people are wrong. Not because they're dishonest or unkind, but because they've never actually examined how they communicate. They speak the way they've always spoken, listen the way they've always listened, and then wonder why certain conversations keep going sideways.

Purposeful communication is different. It's the practice of speaking with clarity and intention, listening with genuine curiosity, and making sure the message you're sending is actually the message being received. That last part is where most breakdowns happen. You meant one thing. They heard another. Neither of you realized it until the damage was already done.

Your words, your tone, and your body language all send signals simultaneously. When they're aligned, your message lands clean. When they're not, people trust what they see and feel over what you say. You can tell someone you're not frustrated while your jaw is tight and your responses are clipped. They won't believe the words. They'll believe the jaw. This is why self-awareness, the skill you've been building since Phase 2, is so directly relevant to communication. You can't align your signals if you don't know what they are.

Consider a hypothetical scenario: imagine someone like Jordan, a 36-year-old team lead who prided himself on being direct. He thought directness was a strength, and in many ways it was. But he'd received feedback from two separate team members that conversations with him felt like being cross-examined. He was confused. He wasn't trying to interrogate anyone. He was just asking questions and getting to the point. When he actually watched a recording of one of his one-on-ones, he saw it immediately. His posture was closed. His questions came rapid-fire without any pause for the other person to think. His follow-up responses often started with "right, but" which signaled to the other person that he'd already decided the answer before they finished speaking. He wasn't being malicious. He just hadn't paid attention to the full picture of how he was coming across. Once he saw it, he could change it. He started slowing down. He started leaving space after questions. He started replacing "right, but" with "that's interesting, tell me more." Within a month, the quality of his team conversations had shifted noticeably. Same intention. Completely different delivery.

Active listening is the most underused communication skill in professional life. Not passive listening, where you wait for your turn to speak. Active listening, where you're fully present with what the other person is saying, you're tracking it, you're curious about it, and you're reflecting it back before you respond. It sounds simple. It's genuinely difficult to do consistently, especially when you're busy, when you think you already know the answer, or when what the other person is saying triggers something in you.

Here's the specific practice. In your next significant conversation, try this sequence. First, listen without forming your response until the other person has fully stopped speaking. Second, wait three seconds before you say anything. Third, before you share your own view, say back what you heard in your own words: "So what I'm hearing is..." and finish the sentence. Then ask: "Did I get that right?" That one move, reflecting before responding, prevents more misunderstandings than almost any other communication habit you could build. It also tells the other person something important: that you were actually listening. That signal alone changes the entire tone of the conversation.

Assumptions are the silent destroyers of good communication. You assume you know what someone meant before they've finished explaining. You assume you know why someone did something before you've asked. You assume the other person understands your context when they're working from completely different information. Every assumption is a closed door. Every question is an open one. The quality of your questions, as this takeover has emphasized before, shapes the quality of what you understand. Ask more. Assume less. That's not just a communication principle. It's a relationship practice.

Speaking your truth with clarity and kindness is the other side of this. Being honest doesn't mean being blunt. It means saying what you actually think and feel in a way that respects both yourself and the other person. The formula that works in almost every situation is this: describe the specific behavior or situation, explain how it affects you, and make a clear request. "When the deadline changes without notice, I lose confidence in the plan and spend time redoing work. I'd like to be looped in before changes are finalized." That's honest. That's specific. That's kind. It's not a complaint. It's a communication.

Conflict and Resolution

Conflict is not the problem. Avoidance is.

Most people treat disagreement as something to get through as quickly as possible, to smooth over, to de-escalate before it gets uncomfortable. And so they say less than they mean, agree to things they don't agree with, and walk away from conversations with unresolved tension that quietly builds into resentment. The conflict didn't go away. It just went underground. And underground conflicts are significantly harder to resolve than the ones you face directly.

Real conflict, handled well, does something surprising. It deepens connection. When two people can disagree honestly, work through it without tearing each other apart, and come out the other side with more understanding than they had going in, the relationship is stronger for it. They've proven to each other that it can survive honesty. That proof is one of the most important things a relationship can have.

The key is how you enter the conflict. If you go in to win, you'll almost certainly lose something more important than the argument. If you go in to understand, you have a real chance of both resolving the issue and strengthening the relationship in the process. That shift, from winning to understanding, is the most important move in any difficult conversation.

Think about this practically. Before any hard conversation, ask yourself one question: what outcome do I actually want here? Not what do I want to say. What do I want to have happen when this conversation is over? If the answer is "I want the other person to admit they were wrong," you're going in to win. If the answer is "I want us both to understand each other better and figure out a path forward," you're going in to resolve. Those two starting points produce completely different conversations.

Emotional triggers show up most intensely in conflict. When someone says something that lands wrong, when you feel dismissed or disrespected or cornered, the physiological response is fast. Your chest tightens. Your thinking narrows. The part of your brain that's good at nuance and empathy goes partly offline. This is the moment that determines everything about how the conflict goes. If you react from that triggered state, you'll almost certainly say something that escalates rather than resolves. If you pause, breathe, and come back to your intention, you have a chance to actually get somewhere.

Use the three-breath pause from Phase 2 here. When you feel the trigger fire in a conflict, stop before you speak. Three slow breaths. Then ask yourself: "What do I actually want to happen here?" That question brings you back to your intention. It reminds you that you're not here to win. You're here to understand and be understood.

The approach that works for almost every difficult conversation follows a simple structure. Start by acknowledging the other person's perspective before you share your own. Not agreeing with it. Acknowledging it. "I hear that you felt left out of that decision. That makes sense." Then share your own experience from a first-person perspective: "From my side, I didn't realize you wanted to be included until after it was done." Then move to a specific question about what would help going forward: "What would you need from me in similar situations?" That structure, acknowledge, share, ask, keeps the conversation forward-moving rather than circular.

You don't have to agree to understand. That's one of the most important principles in this entire chapter. You can fully understand why someone sees something the way they do, you can validate that their experience is real and makes sense given their history and perspective, without agreeing that they're right. Understanding isn't concession. It's connection. And connection is what makes resolution possible.

Some conflicts won't resolve in a single conversation. That's okay. What matters is that you keep the channel open. That you don't let a hard conversation become a wall. That you leave every difficult interaction with at least one concrete next step, however small, that moves things forward. "Can we talk about this again on Thursday when we've both had some time to think?" is a next step. "Let me look into what actually happened and get back to you by end of week" is a next step. Forward motion, even slow forward motion, is always better than letting things sit and harden.

The Circle of Influence Audit

There's a principle that's been woven through this takeover since the early weeks: your environment shapes you more than your intentions do. You can have the best values, the clearest purpose, and the strongest habits, and still be quietly pulled off course by the people you spend the most time with. Not through any dramatic influence. Through the slow, constant accumulation of what's normal in your immediate circle.

The people closest to you set the standard for what's acceptable, what's ambitious, what's worth worrying about, and what's possible. If everyone around you treats mediocrity as the ceiling, you'll feel the pull of that ceiling even if you consciously reject it. If the people you spend the most time with are growing, challenging themselves, and holding themselves to a high standard, you'll feel the lift of that too. This isn't about judgment. It's about physics. Your environment exerts force. The question is whether that force is pushing you toward your superior self or away from it.

The Circle of Influence Audit is a structured reflection exercise that makes this visible. It takes about twenty minutes and produces information that most people have been avoiding because it requires honesty about people they care about.

Here's how to do it. Open your journal and write the names of the five people you spend the most time with. Not the five people you like most or the five you wish you spent more time with. The actual five. The ones who take up the most real estate in your daily life, through in-person time, calls, texts, or regular interaction. Write their names in a column.

Next to each name, answer four specific questions. First: when I'm around this person, do I feel more energized or more drained? Second: does spending time with this person make me more likely or less likely to pursue my goals? Third: does this person challenge me to grow, or do they reinforce my current limitations? Fourth: when I imagine the person I'm becoming through this takeover, does this relationship support that version of me or create friction with it?

Be honest. This isn't about finding reasons to cut people out of your life. Most relationships are more complex than a simple positive or negative rating. Someone can drain your energy in certain contexts and be genuinely important to you in others. A family member might not support your ambitions but still be someone you love and choose to stay close to. The audit isn't a verdict. It's information.

What you're looking for are patterns. Are most of the five people on your list pulling you toward growth or away from it? Is there someone on the list who consistently leaves you feeling smaller, less capable, or more doubtful after interactions? Is there someone who's missing from your daily life who should be there more? Someone who challenges you, believes in you, and reflects back the version of yourself you're trying to become?

Think about a hypothetical scenario: imagine someone like Marcus, a 32-year-old entrepreneur who had been in the same social circle since his mid-twenties. He genuinely liked these people. But when he did this audit honestly, he noticed something uncomfortable. Every time he shared a new idea or a goal he was working toward, the response from most of his circle was some version of skepticism or gentle discouragement. "That's risky." "Are you sure that's realistic?" "What if it doesn't work out?" None of them were being malicious. They were expressing genuine concern from their own risk-averse worldview. But Marcus was absorbing that worldview every time they talked. He wasn't cutting anyone off. He did start being more intentional about who he shared his goals with and who he spent time with when he needed encouragement rather than caution. He also made one specific change: he reached out to a mentor he'd been meaning to reconnect with for over a year. That one relationship, reactivated, changed the quality of his thinking more than any other single action he took that month.

Curating your environment doesn't mean surrounding yourself only with people who agree with everything you do. That's not a circle of influence. That's an echo chamber. What you're looking for is people who challenge you toward growth, not people who challenge you toward doubt. People who hold you accountable with care, not people who undermine you with criticism. People who are genuinely invested in your development, not just comfortable with your current level.

Once you've completed the audit, take two specific actions. First, identify the one person in your current circle who most consistently pulls you toward your superior self. Reach out to them this week. Not with a specific agenda. Just to connect. Tell them they matter to you. Ask how they're doing. Invest in that relationship deliberately, because it's one of your most valuable assets.

Second, identify one person who's been missing from your circle, someone who's further along than you in an area you're working on, someone whose perspective and experience would genuinely help you grow. This might be a mentor, a peer in a different field, someone you admire from a distance but have never actually approached. Reach out to them this week with one specific, honest message. Tell them what you're working on. Tell them why their perspective would be valuable. Ask for thirty minutes of their time. The worst they can say is no. The best outcome is a relationship that changes the trajectory of your next year.

Your circle is either an anchor or a sail. It's either holding you in place or helping you move. You get to decide which relationships to invest in more and which ones to be more intentional about. That's not disloyalty. That's self-leadership applied to your social life. And it's one of the most powerful levers available to you in the final stretch of this takeover.

Relationships are where everything you've built in this takeover gets tested in real time. Your self-awareness gets tested when someone triggers you in a meeting. Your values get tested when a friendship asks you to compromise what you believe. Your resilience gets tested when a relationship goes through a hard stretch. Your communication skills get tested every single day in every conversation you have. This phase isn't separate from the work you've been doing. It's the arena where that work becomes visible.

The three actions below are specific, concrete, and designed to produce real outcomes in your actual relationships starting today.

Action Step 1: Set one firm boundary with someone who drains your energy. Go back to your Circle of Influence Audit. Identify one relationship where you consistently leave interactions feeling depleted, resentful, or smaller than when you arrived. Choose one specific behavior in that relationship that you're no longer willing to accept without addressing. Then communicate the boundary clearly, calmly, and without over-explaining. Use the formula: describe the specific situation, explain how it affects you, make a clear request. Do this within the next 48 hours. Not eventually. Not when the timing feels perfect. Within 48 hours. Write down what you're going to say before you say it. Practice it out loud once. Then have the conversation. Notice how it feels to protect your energy with clarity rather than resentment.

Action Step 2: Reach out to a mentor or an inspiring peer. Identify one person whose perspective, experience, or way of operating genuinely inspires you. Someone who's navigating life at a level you're working toward. Write them a message today. Keep it short and honest. Tell them what you're working on. Tell them specifically what you'd value about their perspective. Ask for thirty minutes of their time, in person, by phone, or by video. Don't wait until you feel ready or until you have the perfect thing to say. Send the message today. The act of reaching out is itself an expression of the growth mindset you've been building. People who are where you want to be almost always remember what it was like to be where you are. Most of them are more willing to help than you assume.

Action Step 3: Practice active listening in your next social interaction. Before your next significant conversation, write this at the top of your notes or say it to yourself: "Listen first. Understand before I respond." Then do exactly that. Put your phone away. Make eye contact. Let the other person finish completely before you speak. After they finish, wait three full seconds. Then reflect back what you heard before sharing your own view. Do this once today and write down two sentences about what shifted in the quality of the conversation when you were fully present for it. Repeat this in every significant conversation for the remainder of this week. By day seven, notice whether it's starting to feel less effortful and more natural.

The relationships in your life are not background scenery. They're the context in which your superior self either shows up or stays hidden. Every conversation is a chance to practice what you've built. Every conflict is a chance to choose understanding over winning. Every boundary you set is a vote for the version of yourself that respects their own energy. Every connection you deepen is an investment in the life you're designing.

You're six days from the end of this takeover. The relationships you're building and refining right now aren't just part of week thirteen. They're the infrastructure of everything that comes after it. Build them with the same intention you've brought to every other phase of this work.

Phase 14: Legacy and Lifelong Growth

You made it to day 92.

Ninety-two days ago, you sat down with a blank page and a commitment you weren't entirely sure you could keep. You wrote your intention. You said it out loud. And then you showed up, day after day, through the phases that were uncomfortable, through the weeks where motivation disappeared, through the moments where the old version of you pushed back hard against the new one being built. That's not a small thing. That's the entire point of everything this takeover was designed to do.

But here's what this final phase is really about. It's not a victory lap. It's not a summary of what you've already learned. It's the question that all 91 days before it were quietly building toward: now that you've done this work on yourself, what are you going to do with it? Who else gets to benefit from the person you've become? And how do you make sure this growth doesn't stop when the 98 days do?

Those three questions are the entire substance of Phase 14. Legacy. Mentorship. Celebration. And the commitment to keep going long after this takeover ends.

Defining Your Legacy

Most people think of legacy as something that gets decided after they're gone. A eulogy. A plaque. The memories people share at a funeral. That framing makes legacy feel distant and abstract, like something you earn over a lifetime and only find out about at the end. It also makes it feel passive, like something that happens to you rather than something you build.

That framing is wrong. And replacing it with something more accurate is one of the most useful things you can do right now.

Your legacy is being built today. Right now. In how you show up for the people around you. In the standard you hold yourself to when no one's watching. In the ripple effects of every conversation you have, every decision you make, every person you encourage or challenge or help move forward. Legacy isn't a final destination. It's a daily practice. And the person you've been becoming through these 98 days has been building it all along, whether you named it that way or not.

Think about the people who have had the most lasting impact on your life. The teacher who saw something in you that you didn't see yet. The manager who gave you real feedback when everyone else just nodded along. The friend who told you the truth when you needed it most. The parent, the mentor, the colleague who showed up consistently in a way that made you feel like you mattered. None of those people were famous. None of them had monuments built in their honor. But their impact is real, and it's still running in you right now. That's legacy. Quiet, specific, and built through daily action over time.

The mark you leave on your industry, your family, and your community doesn't require a grand gesture. It requires clarity about what you stand for and the discipline to live that out consistently. You've been building both of those things since day one of this takeover. The values you named in Phase 5. The identity you mapped in Phase 3. The leadership you developed in Phase 8. The purpose you clarified in Phase 12. All of it feeds directly into the legacy you're already creating.

Now it's time to name it deliberately.

Consider a hypothetical scenario: imagine someone like Elise, a 37-year-old operations director who went through a takeover similar to this one. When she first sat down to think about legacy, she felt stuck. She wasn't famous. She hadn't invented anything. She didn't run a massive company. She almost dismissed the whole exercise as irrelevant to someone at her level. Then she thought about what her team members had said to her over the years. How she was the first manager who ever asked them what they actually wanted from their careers. How she ran meetings where people felt safe enough to disagree. How she'd fought internally for resources for her team when it would have been easier to stay quiet. That was her legacy. Not a headline. A pattern of behavior that made the people around her feel valued and capable. When she saw it clearly, she stopped treating it as accidental and started treating it as intentional. She started asking herself every day: am I adding to this or subtracting from it?

That question, "am I adding to this or subtracting from it?", is the most practical legacy question you can ask. It's specific enough to guide daily behavior and broad enough to apply to everything.

Here is the specific exercise for defining your legacy right now. Open your journal and write the heading: "How I want to be remembered." Then write freely for ten minutes. Don't write what sounds impressive. Don't write what you think you should say. Write what actually moves you when you sit with the question honestly. How do you want the people who worked alongside you to describe you? How do you want your family to feel because you were present in their lives? What do you want to have contributed to your field, your community, or the people you've led and mentored? What problems do you want to have helped solve? What kind of person do you want to have been?

When you're done, read what you wrote. Circle the three things that feel most true and most important. Those three things are the core of your legacy statement. Now write one clear sentence that captures all three. Start it with: "I want to be remembered as someone who..." That sentence is your north star for everything that comes after these 98 days. Every major decision you make, every relationship you invest in, every opportunity you take or pass on, you can hold it up against that sentence and ask: does this move me toward this or away from it?

Your legacy isn't fixed. It grows and deepens as you do. But it has to be named before it can be built with intention. You've just named it. Now comes the daily practice of living it.

Mentorship and Influence

There's a specific moment in any growth process where the work stops being purely about you. You've been doing deep, focused internal work for 92 days. You've examined your beliefs, rebuilt your habits, clarified your purpose, and developed the kind of self-awareness that most people spend their whole lives avoiding. That work was necessary. It was also, by design, inward-facing. Phase 14 is where the direction changes.

When you've done real work on yourself, you carry something that other people genuinely need. Not because you have all the answers, but because you've been through the process. You know what the resistance feels like. You know what it takes to push through the dip. You know what it means to examine a limiting belief and choose a different story. That knowledge, lived rather than theoretical, is exactly what someone earlier in their growth needs to hear from someone further along.

That's what mentorship is. Not expertise dispensed from a pedestal. It's honest guidance from someone who's walked a similar road and is willing to share what they found on it.

Mentorship runs in two directions, and both of them matter. Being a mentor means pulling someone else forward. Finding a mentor means allowing someone further along to pull you. Most people are comfortable with one of these and resistant to the other. High achievers often resist finding a mentor because asking for guidance feels like admitting they don't have it figured out. Younger professionals often resist becoming a mentor because they don't feel qualified yet. Both of those resistances are worth examining, because both of them are forms of the same limiting belief: that you have to be fully arrived before you have something worth giving or receiving.

You don't have to be at the end of your growth to mentor someone. You just have to be far enough ahead to see the path more clearly than they can right now. Someone who finished month three of a twelve-month program has something real to offer someone who's just starting month one. You don't need a title, a credential, or a perfectly curated story. You need honesty and the willingness to share it.

Think about a hypothetical scenario: imagine someone like Ray, a 40-year-old sales manager who had spent years telling himself he wasn't "the mentoring type." He was introverted, not naturally given to long conversations about feelings or growth. But a junior colleague named Sofia kept coming to him with questions, not about sales tactics, but about how to handle the pressure, how to stay motivated when the numbers weren't there, how to deal with the self-doubt that came with a tough quarter. Ray started answering her questions honestly, the way he wished someone had answered his questions ten years earlier. He wasn't running formal sessions. He was just being real with her in the ten-minute conversations they had in the hallway or over coffee. Six months later, Sofia was one of the top performers on the team. She told Ray directly that his honesty had changed how she saw herself. He hadn't given her a strategy. He'd given her permission to stop being so hard on herself. That's mentorship. Informal, honest, and genuinely powerful.

Finding a mentor requires the same honesty in the opposite direction. It means identifying someone whose life or work reflects something you're genuinely working toward and being willing to ask for their time and perspective. Not to extract information. To learn from their experience and allow their clarity to sharpen yours.

The best mentoring relationships aren't transactional. They're reciprocal. Even when there's a significant difference in experience, the person being mentored brings fresh questions, new perspectives, and often a clarity of purpose that the mentor finds genuinely energizing. The best mentors will tell you that their mentees teach them as much as they teach their mentees. That exchange is what makes the relationship valuable for both people.

Here is the specific action for this section. You're going to do two things this week, one in each direction of mentorship.

First, identify someone who is earlier in their growth than you are. Not necessarily in years, but in terms of the specific work you've been doing through this takeover. Someone who's struggling with something you've worked through. A colleague who's dealing with the limiting beliefs you've spent the last 92 days dismantling. A friend who's trying to build better habits but doesn't have a system. A younger professional who's trying to find their footing in a role that challenges them. Reach out to this person this week. Tell them honestly that you've been doing some personal growth work and that you'd like to share something that's helped you. Ask if they'd be open to a conversation. Keep it simple. Keep it real. You don't need a curriculum. You just need to show up and be honest about what you've learned.

Second, identify someone who is further along than you in an area you're still developing. This might be someone you admire professionally, someone whose leadership style reflects what you're working toward, someone who has built the kind of relationships or career or life that connects to your legacy statement. Send them a message this week. Tell them specifically what you're working on. Tell them why their perspective would be valuable. Ask for thirty minutes. Be direct and be genuine. Most people who have done real work on themselves are willing to share it with someone who's clearly serious about their own growth. The worst outcome is a polite no. The best outcome is a relationship that shapes the next chapter of your life.

Mentorship is how legacy compounds. When you share what you've learned, it doesn't diminish what you have. It multiplies it. Every person you help move forward carries something of what you gave them into every room they walk into after that. That's the ripple effect. That's how one person's growth becomes something much larger than one person's story.

Celebrating Milestones

You've been in motion for 97 days. And if you're anything like most driven, goal-oriented people, you've already started thinking about what comes next. The next goal. The next phase. The next version of the system. The forward momentum is real and it's valuable. But before you step into what's next, you need to do something that high achievers consistently skip, something that turns out to be more important for long-term growth than almost anything else.

You need to stop and actually feel what you've done.

Not for vanity. Not to broadcast it. But because acknowledging your progress is one of the most powerful things you can do for the sustainability of your growth. When you move from goal to goal without pausing to register what you've accomplished, you're training your brain to treat achievement as invisible. And when achievement is invisible, the effort required to reach it starts to feel meaningless. That's one of the quieter causes of burnout among high-performing people. They keep pushing but stop feeling like any of it is landing. The celebration isn't a reward. It's a recalibration. It tells your nervous system that the effort was worth it, which makes the next effort more likely to happen.

Transformation is a long game. The 98-Day Superior Self Takeover gave it a structure and a timeline, but the work you've done here doesn't end on day 98. It continues for the rest of your life. And if you want that continuation to be sustainable, you need to build in the practice of acknowledging progress along the way. Not just at the end of a takeover. Regularly. Intentionally. As part of how you operate.

Think about what you've actually done over the past 98 days. You built a daily awareness practice that most people never develop. You examined beliefs you'd been carrying for years and consciously chose different ones. You mapped your identity independent of your job title. You named your core values and started making decisions that actually reflect them. You built habits through a system that works with your brain rather than against it. You developed your leadership from the inside out. You pushed through the dip when everything in you wanted to quit. You clarified your purpose and started living more deliberately toward it. You worked on your relationships with the same intentionality you brought to your internal work. And now you're here, in the final phase, naming your legacy and thinking about how to give what you've built to the world around you.

That's not a small thing. That's a genuinely different person than the one who opened this book on day one.

Celebration doesn't have to be elaborate. It has to be intentional. The form it takes matters less than the act of marking the moment deliberately. For some people, that's a dinner with the people who supported them through the process. For others, it's a solo experience, a trip, a long walk somewhere meaningful, an evening with no agenda and no devices. For others still, it's writing a letter to themselves about what they've done and who they've become. There's no single right way to celebrate. There's only the choice to do it consciously rather than skipping past it.

Here is the specific practice for this section. Do three things before day 98 ends.

First, write a letter to yourself. Address it to the version of you who started this takeover on day one. Tell that person what you've learned. Tell them what was harder than expected and what surprised you. Tell them what you're most proud of. Tell them what you're carrying forward. This isn't a performance. No one else has to read it. Write it honestly, the way you'd write to someone you care about who needed to hear the truth.

When you're done, seal it or save it somewhere you'll find it in six months. Reading it then will tell you something important about how far you've continued to travel.

Second, identify three specific wins from this takeover that you haven't fully acknowledged yet. Not your biggest or most impressive ones. Three real ones that mattered to you personally. The day you had the difficult conversation you'd been avoiding for months. The week you held your morning routine through a genuinely chaotic stretch. The moment you caught a limiting belief in real time and chose a different response. Write them down. Sit with each one for a moment. Let them register as real. These aren't small things. They're evidence of who you've become.

Third, plan a deliberate celebration for completing day 98. Not a vague intention to do something nice. An actual plan. Decide what it is, when it will happen, and who, if anyone, will be part of it. Put it in your calendar right now. Treat it with the same seriousness you'd give a meeting with someone you respect. Because that's exactly what it is: a meeting with the version of yourself you've spent 98 days building. Show up for it.

Celebrating milestones is also how you maintain the motivation required for lifelong growth beyond this takeover. The 98 days gave you a structure. The structure ends. The growth doesn't have to. But growth without acknowledgment is exhausting. It becomes a treadmill with no finish line. Building the habit of pausing to register your progress, at the end of a takeover, at the end of a hard week, at the end of a year, is what keeps the long game sustainable. It's what separates people who grow for a season from people who keep growing for a lifetime.

Your Next Move

You've reached the final section of the 98-Day Superior Self Takeover. Everything in this book, every phase, every micro-action, every reflection prompt, every uncomfortable question, has been building toward this moment. Not the end of the work. The beginning of what the work was always for.

The shift from personal growth to collective impact is the natural next step for someone who has done what you've done. You didn't go through 98 days of this to keep it to yourself. The self-awareness, the habits, the values clarity, the leadership, the resilience, the purpose, none of it reaches its full potential in isolation. It reaches its full potential when it flows outward, into your work, your relationships, your community, and the people who will be shaped by who you've become.

That's the full picture of what total life redesign actually means. Not just a better version of you in a vacuum. A better version of you in the world, making the world around you better in the specific, quiet, daily ways that add up to something real over time.

Three actions to complete before you close this book.

The first action: write down how you want to be remembered. Use the exercise from the first section of this chapter. Write the full ten-minute reflection. Circle the three things that matter most. Write your one-sentence legacy statement. Then put it somewhere visible. Your journal. Your desk. Your phone. Read it every week. Let it be the filter through which you make your most important decisions going forward.

The second action: offer help or guidance to someone earlier in their growth. Use the mentorship practice from the second section. Identify one person who could benefit from something you've learned through this takeover. Reach out to them this week. Have the conversation. Be honest about what you've been through and what you've found on the other side of it. You don't need to have it all figured out. You just need to be willing to share what's real. That willingness is the whole thing.

The third action: plan and execute your day 98 celebration. Make it intentional. Make it specific. Make it something that actually marks the moment rather than just letting it pass. Write the letter to your day-one self. Acknowledge your three wins. Show up for the celebration you planned. Let it land. Let yourself feel what you've done.

The 98-Day Superior Self Takeover doesn't end on day 98. It becomes the foundation you build the rest of your life on. The habits you've built continue. The values you've named continue guiding your decisions. The identity you've constructed continues to deepen. The legacy you've defined continues to be built, one day at a time, through every choice you make about how to show up in the world.

You started this because something in you knew you were capable of more. Ninety-eight days later, that's not just something you believe. It's something you've proven. The superior self you've been building isn't a future version of you waiting to arrive. It's the person who showed up on day 92 and every day before it.

That person is who you are now. Take them with you.

Phase 15: The 98-Day Integration

Day 98 is here.

Not as a finish line. As a foundation. Everything you've built over the past fourteen weeks, every belief you've examined, every habit you've stacked, every uncomfortable truth you've sat with, it doesn't get filed away when you close this book. It becomes the ground you stand on for everything that comes next. That's what this final phase is about. Not wrapping up. Locking in.

Before you look forward, you need to look back. Not to relive the journey, but to see the full picture of what you've actually built. Most people finish something significant and immediately move on to the next thing without ever stopping to register what they've done. That's a costly habit. The integration work in this chapter is designed to prevent it.

Reviewing the Visual Progress Map

Pull out your Visual Progress Map right now. If you've been tracking consistently, you're looking at fourteen weeks of checked boxes, reflection notes, and weekly quiz results. If you drifted in some weeks and came back in others, that's on the map too. Either way, what you're holding is a real record of 98 days of intentional effort. That record matters.

The map is divided into two distinct arcs. Weeks one through seven, the B.O.S.S. phase, were about building the foundation. Self-awareness. Identity. Understanding. Values. Passion. Security. These weren't soft concepts. They were the internal infrastructure that everything else in this takeover was built on top of. Weeks eight through fourteen, the B.O.S.S. 2.0 phase, were about taking that foundation and using it to lead, grow, and create something that extends beyond you. Leadership. Habits. Mindset. Resilience. Purpose. Relationships. Legacy.

Look at the map as a whole. Not week by week. As a complete picture.

What you'll likely notice is that the two phases feel different in quality. The first seven weeks probably felt more internal, more reflective, sometimes more uncomfortable. You were doing excavation work. Pulling up things that had been buried. The second seven weeks probably felt more active, more outward-facing, more demanding in a different way. You were building something visible with what you found underground. Both phases were necessary. Neither one works without the other. You can't build strong habits on a foundation you haven't examined. You can't lead others well if you don't know yourself. The map shows you that these weren't fourteen separate weeks. They were one continuous arc.

Now go deeper. Look at each of the fourteen growth zones individually and answer one honest question about each one: what's the single most important thing I learned about myself in this week? Don't overthink it. Write the first honest answer that comes up. By the time you've answered that question fourteen times, you'll have a clear picture of your most significant growth edges, the places where the work changed something real, and the places where you still have more to develop.

Week one asked you to choose your superior self deliberately. Week two asked you to see yourself in real time without judgment. Week three asked you to separate who you are from what you do. Week four asked you to listen more than you speak and to question what you assume. Week five asked you to name what you actually stand for and make decisions that reflect it. Week six asked you to stop waiting for passion to find you and start moving toward it. Week seven asked you to build a sense of worth that doesn't depend on anyone else's approval.

Then the second arc began. Week eight asked you to lead yourself before you tried to lead anyone else. Week nine asked you to build your habits with precision, not willpower. Week ten asked you to examine the beliefs running your mind and replace the ones that don't serve you. Week eleven asked you to absorb setbacks as data rather than verdicts. Week twelve asked you to name your why and start living toward it. Week thirteen asked you to show up honestly in your relationships and set the boundaries that protect your energy. Week fourteen asked you to define your legacy and start building it today.

Fourteen weeks. Fourteen growth zones. One person, built deliberately, one day at a time.

Think about a hypothetical scenario: imagine someone like Dara, a 33-year-old product manager who started this takeover feeling competent at her job but hollow underneath it. She could hit her targets, manage her team, and keep everything moving forward. But she felt like she was performing a version of herself rather than actually being herself. When she reviewed her completed Visual Progress Map at day 98, she noticed something she hadn't expected. The weeks that had felt the most uncomfortable, the identity work in week three and the values conflict work in week five, had produced the most lasting change. The weeks she'd been most excited about at the start, the leadership content, the habit systems, had only clicked because the earlier, harder work had cleared the ground for them. The map made that sequence visible in a way that reading about it never could have. She could see her own growth laid out in front of her. That visibility changed how she understood what she'd done. It wasn't just that she'd finished a takeover. She'd built something real, and she could see exactly how she'd built it.

Your map tells a similar story. The specific details are yours. The structure of the growth is universal.

Once you've answered the one-question reflection for each of the fourteen weeks, do one final step with the map. Put a star next to the three growth zones where you feel the most work is still ahead of you. Not the ones you failed at. The ones where you made real progress but can see clearly that there's more to develop. Those three zones are your priority focus areas for the next chapter of your growth. You'll come back to them in the B.O.S.S. 2.0 planning work in the next section.

Celebrate each milestone you see on that map. Not performatively. Genuinely. Every check mark represents a day you chose to show up when you could have chosen not to. Every reflection entry represents a moment of honesty you could have avoided. Every quiz you completed represents a willingness to be measured rather than to coast. Those aren't small things. They're the substance of real change.

Journal your wins from the map before you move forward. Write at least one paragraph about what you're most proud of from these 98 days. Not the most impressive thing. The most real thing. The moment that surprised you. The week you pushed through when you were certain you couldn't. The belief you actually changed. The boundary you finally set. Write it down. Let it land. Then carry it with you into what comes next.

Maintaining the B.O.S.S. Lifestyle

The 98-Day Superior Self Takeover ends on day 98. The B.O.S.S. lifestyle doesn't.

This is the most important distinction in this entire chapter. The takeover was a structure designed to create a new baseline. The habits, the mindset practices, the self-awareness routines, the boundary-setting, the values-based decision-making, none of that was meant to be temporary. It was meant to become how you operate. Permanently. The 98 days gave you the container. What you built inside it is yours to keep.

But keeping it requires intention. Growth that isn't maintained tends to drift. Not dramatically. Quietly. A morning routine that gets skipped for one week becomes skipped for two. A self-awareness practice that gets deprioritized during a busy month gets forgotten entirely by month three. The habits you've built are real, but they're not yet so deeply ingrained that they'll sustain themselves without any attention. You need a maintenance system. Not a new takeover. A set of daily, weekly, and monthly practices that keep the foundation solid.

Start with your daily anchor practices. There are four of them, and they take less than fifteen minutes combined. The first is the Centering Breath Exercise. You've been using this since the introduction. Five slow breaths before you start your day's work. Four counts in, six counts out. This isn't optional maintenance. It's the practice that keeps your nervous system regulated and your attention intentional rather than reactive. Do it every morning without negotiation. Before your phone. Before your email. Before anything else.

The second daily anchor is your gratitude list. Three specific things you're grateful for, written down each morning. Not general. Specific. You learned in Phase 10 that this practice literally changes how your brain scans the environment throughout the day. It trains your reticular activating system to find what's working rather than defaulting to what's missing. Three minutes. Every morning. This is one of the highest-return practices in the entire takeover, and it's one of the easiest to let slide because it feels too simple to matter. It's not too simple. Do it.

The third daily anchor is your self-respect inventory. Three specific things you genuinely respect about yourself today. Not accomplishments. Qualities, choices, behaviors. You built this practice in Phase 7 as the foundation of genuine self-security. It's also the practice that keeps your identity grounded and stable when external circumstances get unstable. Keep it going.

The fourth daily anchor is the Body Scan Meditation. Three to five minutes, slowly bringing your awareness from your head to your toes, noticing what's present without judging it. This practice keeps you connected to your body's signals, the early warning system for stress, triggers, and emotional states that are building before you've consciously registered them. It grounds you in the present moment before the day pulls your attention in twenty directions at once.

These four practices together take less than fifteen minutes. They're the minimum viable maintenance for the B.O.S.S. lifestyle. If you do nothing else from this chapter, do these four things every morning for the next 98 days. The compounding effect of fifteen intentional minutes at the start of each day is not small. Over months and years, it becomes the difference between someone who grew during a takeover and someone who keeps growing for the rest of their life.

Beyond the daily anchors, maintain a weekly rhythm. Once a week, spend twenty minutes reviewing your Visual Progress Map or a simplified version of it. Ask yourself three questions: what did I do this week that aligned with my values? Where did I drift from the person I'm committed to being? What's one specific adjustment I'll make next week? This weekly review doesn't have to be elaborate. Twenty minutes of honest reflection once a week is enough to catch drift before it becomes a pattern.

Your accountability structure from Phase 9 should continue. Keep the weekly check-in with your accountability partner. Keep it short. Keep it honest. What did you commit to? What did you do? What are you committing to next week? That structure, maintained beyond the takeover, is one of the most reliable predictors of whether the growth you've made sticks or slowly fades.

Think about a hypothetical scenario: imagine someone like Marcus, a 37-year-old operations director who finished a 90-day personal development program three years before doing this takeover. He'd made real progress during that program. He'd felt genuinely different by the end of it. But within six months of finishing, almost everything had drifted back. Not through any dramatic failure. Through the slow erosion of not having a maintenance system. He'd told himself he'd "remember what he learned." He hadn't. When he finished this takeover, he made a different choice. He scheduled his four daily anchor practices into his calendar as non-negotiable appointments. He kept his weekly check-in with his accountability partner. He set a calendar reminder every three months to do a full review of his values, his habits, and his progress map. That structure, simple as it sounds, is what made the difference. Two years later, the growth he made during the 98 days is still compounding. Not because he's perfect. Because he built a system that doesn't require perfection to function.

The B.O.S.S. lifestyle is also maintained through your environment. The people you spend time with, the content you consume, the physical spaces you inhabit, all of it either supports your growth or quietly works against it. You did the Circle of Influence Audit in Phase 13. Keep applying its principles. Keep being intentional about who you give your energy to and what you allow into your daily mental environment. Your environment is always exerting force. Make sure it's still pushing in the right direction.

One more thing about maintenance that most people miss: it has to include recovery. You can't operate at a high level indefinitely without building in genuine rest. Not passive scrolling. Not half-present downtime. Real recovery. Sleep. Physical movement. Time in nature. Time with people who restore rather than drain you. Time doing something that has nothing to do with productivity or growth. These aren't indulgences. They're the fuel that makes sustained high performance possible. Without recovery, even the best maintenance system eventually breaks down. Build it in deliberately.

The B.O.S.S. lifestyle isn't a state you achieve. It's a practice you maintain. The distinction matters because it removes the pressure of having to be perfect and replaces it with the simpler, more sustainable requirement of showing up consistently. You don't have to be a different person every day. You just have to keep being the person you've built over these 98 days, with the same intention, the same honesty, and the same willingness to keep doing the small things that make the big things possible.

Recap and Actionable Steps

You started this takeover with a question, even if you didn't phrase it that way at the time. The question was: who am I capable of becoming if I show up for myself every single day for 98 days? You now have the answer. Not as a theory. As lived evidence.

The 14-week arc of the B.O.S.S. takeover was designed to do something specific. It was designed to take someone who was competent, capable, and quietly stuck, and give them the tools, the structure, and the daily practice to become someone genuinely different. Not different in a cosmetic way. Different at the level of how they see themselves, how they make decisions, how they show up for other people, and what they believe is possible for their life.

That's what you've done. And now the work is to make sure it doesn't stop here.

The three action steps below are the final ones this takeover asks of you. They're also the most forward-looking ones. They're not about reviewing what you've done. They're about deciding what you're going to do with it.

Action Step 1: Review your initial "why" and see how it has evolved. Go back to the very first piece of writing you did in this takeover. The intention you set on day one. The sentence you wrote about what you were committing to and why it mattered. Read it now. Then write a response to it from where you stand today. How has your understanding of your "why" deepened over 98 days? What did you think you were working toward at the start that you now understand differently? What surprised you about what actually changed? Write at least one full paragraph. Be specific. The gap between who you were when you wrote the original intention and who you are now reading it is the most concrete measure of your growth available to you. Don't skip this step. It's the one that makes the whole 98 days coherent.

Action Step 2: Commit to a B.O.S.S. 2.0 plan for the next 98 days. The takeover ends. Your growth doesn't. The B.O.S.S. 2.0 plan is your personal continuation structure for the next 98 days. Here's exactly how to build it. First, take the three growth zones you starred on your Visual Progress Map, the ones where you see the most work still ahead. These become your primary focus areas for the next 98 days. Second, for each of the three zones, write one specific habit or practice you'll maintain or deepen over the next 98 days. Make it concrete. Not "I'll work on my mindset." Name the exact practice, the exact frequency, and the exact trigger that will cue it. Third, identify one new challenge you'll take on in the next 98 days that pushes you into territory you haven't entered yet. Something that connects to your legacy statement and your purpose work from Phases 12 and 14. Write it down as a commitment, not an intention. Sign it. Date it. Put it somewhere you'll see it every week. The B.O.S.S. 2.0 plan isn't a new takeover. It's the bridge between the structure you've just completed and the self-directed growth that continues for the rest of your life. Build it with the same specificity you brought to every other phase of this work.

Action Step 3: Join the online community to stay connected with other high-performers. Go to www.weinspireonline.com and sign in or create your account. This isn't optional maintenance. It's infrastructure. The community is where you'll find other people who have done this work, who understand what the dip feels like, who know what it means to push through week nine when the novelty is gone and the finish line isn't visible yet. These are people who speak your language now. Connect with them. Share your experience from the 98 days. Ask a specific question about something you're still working through. Offer something from what you've learned to someone who's earlier in the process than you are. The B.O.S.S. community isn't a passive resource. It's an active environment that makes your continued growth more likely and more sustainable. Use it the way you used your accountability partner during the takeover: honestly, consistently, and with real investment in the exchange.

The 98-Day Superior Self Takeover was built on one foundational truth: small, consistent actions, compounded over time, produce transformation that grand gestures never could. You've lived that truth for 98 days. You've felt it in the weeks where nothing seemed to be changing and then suddenly something shifted. You've seen it in the Visual Progress Map that shows, check mark by check mark, a person showing up for themselves every single day.

That truth doesn't expire on day 98. It's available to you every day for the rest of your life. The takeover gave it structure. Now you carry it forward as a practice, as a way of operating, as the baseline of who you are.

The superior self you've been building isn't finished. Growth that's worth having is never finished. But the foundation is solid. The tools are yours. The identity is real. And the next 98 days, and the 98 after that, belong to the person you've proven you're capable of being.

That person showed up on day one. They showed up every day after. They're showing up right now.

Conclusion

The New You: A Summary of the Journey

Ninety-eight days ago, you made a decision. You didn't just pick up a book. You chose to stop letting your life happen to you by default and started building it with intention. That choice, made once and then again every single morning, is what brought you here.

Think about where you started. You had a vague sense that something needed to change. Maybe it was a feeling you couldn't quite name. Maybe it was the Sunday dread, the hollow performance, the gap between who you were showing up as and who you knew you were capable of being. You had desire. What you didn't have was a system. The 98-Day Superior Self Takeover gave you that system, and you used it.

Look at what you've actually built.

In Phase 1, you stopped treating your choices as isolated moments and started seeing them as votes for the person you're becoming. You set a specific vision, examined your limiting beliefs, and made your first real declaration of who you're committed to being. That wasn't warm-up work. That was the foundation everything else was built on.

Phase 2 gave you something most people never develop: the ability to catch yourself in the act. You learned to notice your thoughts, your triggers, and your self-talk in real time rather than hours after the fact. That awareness, practiced daily through the three check-ins and the self-talk audit, is the skill that makes every other skill in this takeover possible. You can't change what you can't see. Now you can see it.

Phase 3 asked you to strip away every label and look at who you actually are underneath them. That's harder than it sounds for someone who has spent years defining themselves by their title, their role, or their results. You did it anyway. You mapped your identity, traced your generational layers, and started writing a new personal narrative, one you chose rather than one that was handed to you by default.

Phases 4 and 5 moved your attention outward. You cleaned your perceptual lens and started seeing people more accurately. You named your non-negotiables and learned to make decisions that actually reflect what you stand for. You stopped living by values you inherited without questioning and started living by values you consciously chose.

Phase 6 asked you to stop waiting for passion to arrive and start moving toward what already lights you up. Phase 7 moved your sense of worth from the outside to the inside. These two phases together changed something fundamental: you stopped needing the world to confirm your value before you could function well in it.

Then B.O.S.S. 2.0 began. Phase 8 turned everything inward-facing into something that flows outward. You developed your leadership not through a title or an authority structure, but through the quality of your presence, your consistency, and your genuine investment in the people around you. Phase 9 built the architecture of your daily life with precision. Not through willpower. Through systems that work with your brain rather than against it.

Phase 10 changed the operating system. The mindset work, the growth orientation, the visualization, the gratitude practice, these aren't motivational add-ons. They're the beliefs and practices that determine what you attempt, how you respond when things go wrong, and whether you keep going. You changed them deliberately. That's rare.

Phase 11 built your resilience and grit not as personality traits you either have or don't, but as capacities you developed through specific, repeated practice. You learned to absorb a hit without letting it become a verdict. You learned to push through the dip without needing motivation to do it. You learned to extract the lesson from failure instead of running from it.

Phase 12 answered the deepest question this takeover asks: not what you do or how you do it, but why any of it matters to you. You named your purpose. You started living toward it. That's not a small thing. Most people spend their entire careers without doing it.

Phase 13 brought everything into the arena where it gets tested every single day: your relationships. You built the communication skills that create real connection. You set boundaries rooted in values rather than mood. You audited the people around you and made intentional choices about where to invest your energy. Phase 14 asked you to look beyond yourself entirely and start thinking about the mark you're leaving on the world around you.

And Phase 15 gave you the integration tools to make sure none of this stays temporary.

That's 98 days of real work. Not reading. Not highlighting. Not planning to start. Doing.

Your identity is a choice. Your habits are your architecture. Your resilience is your greatest asset. You've now lived all three of those statements rather than just reading them. The B.O.S.S. takeover didn't give you a new version of yourself. It gave you the tools to build one. You did the building.

Take the Leap into Your Legacy

The takeover is complete. Your life is not.

Everything you've built over these 98 days, the self-awareness, the habits, the values clarity, the leadership, the purpose, it's only as valuable as what you do with it from here. A foundation is only meaningful when something gets built on top of it. You have a foundation now. The question is what you're going to build.

The momentum you've created is real. Momentum is also perishable. It doesn't sustain itself without continued action. The people who finish a takeover like this and then quietly drift back to their old patterns aren't lazy or uncommitted. They just stop treating their growth as a daily practice. They cross the finish line and put down the tools. Don't do that.

Take the momentum you've built and point it at your biggest, most specific goal. Not a vague aspiration. The actual thing. The career move you've been circling for two years. The business you've been "almost ready" to start. The relationship you've been meaning to repair. The creative project you've been protecting yourself from by never fully starting it. Name it. Write it down. Give it a deadline. Then take the first concrete step toward it before this week is over.

The outcome of this work isn't a certificate or a sense of completion. It's a life that actually reflects who you are and what you care about. A career that draws on your real strengths and connects to your genuine purpose. Relationships that are honest, boundaried, and genuinely nourishing. A daily experience that feels like expression rather than performance. That's what authentic fulfillment actually looks like. Not a feeling that arrives and stays forever. A daily practice of living in alignment with what you've named as true and important.

You have the tools. You have the roadmap. You have 98 days of proof that you can do hard things consistently. The only thing left is to keep going.

Think about what you'd say to someone like yourself six months from now, someone who finished this takeover and then let it fade. You'd probably say: go back. Pick it back up. The work was real. Don't let it become a memory instead of a practice. Say that to yourself right now. Then make the choice that keeps it a practice.

The superior self you've been building isn't a destination you arrive at and stay in. It's a direction you keep moving in. Every day you show up, make intentional choices, and live by the values you've named, you're being that person. Not perfectly. Consistently. That's the whole thing.

Your Step-by-Step Path Forward

The takeover gave you a structure. Now you need to carry that structure forward in a form that fits your actual life beyond these 98 days. The five practices below aren't suggestions. They're the specific, daily and ongoing actions that keep everything you've built alive and growing. Each one is concrete. Each one has a clear outcome. Do them in order, and do them consistently.

Step 1: Continue the daily Centering Breath and Intention Setting rituals every single morning. This is non-negotiable. Before your phone, before your email, before the day starts pulling your attention in every direction, sit down for five minutes and do both practices. The Centering Breath takes ninety seconds. Five slow breaths, four counts in, six counts out. This regulates your nervous system and shifts you from reactive mode into intentional mode. The Intention Setting takes three minutes. Write one sentence about what you're committing to today that connects to your larger purpose. Not a to-do list. One sentence about who you're choosing to be today. These two practices together cost you five minutes and change the quality of everything that follows. They're the anchor of the B.O.S.S. lifestyle. If you only keep one thing from this takeover, keep this.

Step 2: Keep using the Visual Progress Map for your next set of goals. Don't put the map away. Adapt it. Take the same structure, weekly themes, daily check-ins, weekly reflections, and apply it to your next 98-day focus. Go back to the three growth zones you starred during your Phase 15 review. Those are your priority areas. Build your next map around them. Give each zone a weekly theme. Give each week a specific micro-action you'll track daily. Check the boxes. Review the map every Sunday for twenty minutes. Ask yourself the same three questions every week: what did I do that aligned with my values, where did I drift, and what's one specific adjustment I'll make next week. The map makes progress visible. Visible progress is what keeps you moving when motivation is thin. Don't stop tracking just because the takeover ended.

Step 3: Regularly audit your Circle of Influence. Do a full Circle of Influence Audit every three months. Not once and done. Every quarter. The people around you shift over time. Your goals shift. What your environment needs to support changes as you grow. Set a calendar reminder right now for 90 days from today. When it goes off, open your journal and answer the same four questions from Phase 13 about the five people you spend the most time with. Are they pulling you toward your superior self or away from it? Adjust accordingly. This doesn't mean cutting people out carelessly. It means being honest about where you're investing your energy and making sure that investment is aligned with who you're becoming. Also, within the next two weeks, reach out to one person who isn't currently in your regular circle but should be. Someone further along than you in an area you're developing. Someone whose presence in your life would raise your standard. Make the ask. Send the message. Build the relationship. Your environment is always shaping you. Keep shaping it back.

Step 4: Stay active in the B.O.S.S. community. Log into www.weinspireonline.com at least once a week. Not to consume. To contribute. Share one specific insight from your 98 days with someone who's earlier in the process than you are. Answer one question someone else has posted. Post one honest update about where you are in your B.O.S.S. 2.0 plan. Teaching what you've learned is the fastest way to deepen your understanding of it. It also keeps you accountable in a way that private practice alone doesn't. When you know you're going to share your progress with a community of people who are doing the same work, you're more likely to actually do the work. That's not a weakness. That's how human beings are wired. Use it. The community is also where you'll find your next accountability partner for the next 98-day cycle. Reach out to someone in the community whose goals and values seem aligned with yours. Set up a weekly ten-minute check-in. Keep it simple. Keep it honest. Keep it going.

Step 5: Never stop asking "What else could be true?" This question, introduced in Phase 4, is the single most powerful tool in this entire takeover for keeping your mind open and your growth continuous. Every time you feel certain about something, about a person, a situation, a belief about yourself, a conclusion you've drawn, ask it. What else could be true? Not to create endless doubt. To create enough space for a better answer to show up. The people who stop growing are almost always the people who stop questioning. They've arrived at their conclusions and they're defending them rather than testing them. You've spent 98 days learning to hold your assumptions more loosely, to stay curious, to ask better questions. Don't stop now. Make this question a permanent part of how you think. Apply it to your career decisions. Apply it to your relationships. Apply it to the stories you tell about yourself when things get hard. The question doesn't have a finish line. It gets more useful the longer you use it. Ask it every day, and your thinking will keep sharpening for the rest of your life.

These five steps aren't a new takeover. They're the distillation of everything the 98-Day Superior Self Takeover built, compressed into a sustainable daily and ongoing practice. They're how you make sure that what you've created over these 98 days doesn't fade into a memory of a time when you briefly tried to change. They're how you make the change permanent.

The version of yourself you've been building through this work isn't finished. It was never supposed to be. Growth that's worth having doesn't have a final form. It deepens, expands, and compounds as long as you keep showing up for it. That's not a burden. That's the whole point. A life of continuous, intentional growth isn't exhausting. It's the most alive you can feel.

You started this because something in you knew you were capable of more. That something was right. Ninety-eight days of proof say so. The superior self you've been building is the person who showed up every day, did the work, and kept going. That's who you are now. That's who you take with you from here.

ACKNOWLEDGMENTS

Writing a book is never a solo act, and this one is no exception. I am deeply grateful to the people who walked alongside me through this journey.

To my editor, Linda Cornett — thank you for your sharp eye, your patience, and your commitment to making every word count. This book is better because of you.

To my Polish Connection — Mark Dobrzycki and Mark Klincewicz — your friendship, loyalty, and support have meant more than words can say. I am grateful for you both.

To my children — Ereatha, Willie, and Michael — you are my greatest accomplishment and my constant reminder of why legacy matters. Everything I do, I do with you in mind.

To my grandchildren — Michael Jr., Nikori, Lakayla, Darneil, and Vanessa — watching you grow into who you are becoming fills me with more pride than I can express. You inspire me every single day.

To my great-grandchildren — Mikai and Markece — you keep me young, keep me smiling, and remind me that the best chapters of this story are still being written.

And a special thank you to my co-keeper, buddy, and friend — Marcus Davis — for your continued inspiration, your positivity, and your unwavering belief in what is possible. You make the work feel lighter and the vision feel reachable. I am grateful to have you in my corner.

ABOUT THE AUTHOR

Larry Barrett is an author, publisher, and storyteller whose work is shaped by more than four decades in music, media, and creative leadership. As the founder of Grin and Barrett Publishing, he writes with depth, purpose, and a deep respect for the power of words to move, challenge, and inspire. His voice reflects a lifelong commitment to legacy, truth, and stories that leave a lasting mark.

For more information, visit larrylbarrett.com or connect with the B.O.S.S. community at weinspireonline.com.

ALSO BY LARRY BARRETT

An American Recipe for Madness Trilogy

A dark, multigenerational crime saga set in Chicago, where trauma becomes legacy, silence becomes survival, and violence echoes across decades. Raw, haunting, and emotionally powerful — this series explores crime, consequence, and the long shadow of what families pass down when healing never comes.

An American Recipe for Madness: The VI-CAP Ghost

Available Now

No Saints in Chicago: Blood Ties and Broken Promises

Coming June 30, 2026

The Devil's Ledger: Final Reckoning

Coming September 30, 2026

Published by Grin and Barrett Publishing

larrylbarrett.com

NOTES

NOTES

NOTES

NOTES

NOTES

NOTES

NOTES

NOTES